Holiness Is
Not Optional

WHAT THE BIBLE TEACHES US
ABOUT NEW COVENANT LIVING

GABRIEL MILLER

ALL PEOPLES MINISTRIES
LYNCHBURG, VA

Holiness is Not Optional: What the Bible Teaches Us About New Covenant Living

Published by All Peoples Ministries
P.O. Box 3034
Lynchburg, Virginia 24503
www.allpeoplesministries.org

Cover design by Samuel C. Petty

ISBN-13: 978-0-9987608-4-1
ISBN-10: 0-9987608-4-6

Printed in the United States of America

To Bowden and Jude. May you far surpass me in holiness.

CONTENTS

The greatest need of the Church of Jesus Christ,
in this critical hour in history, is a baptism of holiness.

-Leonard Ravenhill

INTRODUCTION

If you were to ask me the #1 thing that is lacking in the American Church today, I would say *holiness*. We have doctrine, much of it good. Many know the Bible, many know *about* God. But the average American Christian doesn't really look any different from the average American. We are not holy; we are not set apart.

One of the main reasons holiness is so lacking in the church is that it is no longer preached from our pulpits. It once was. We tend to trace the doctrine of holiness back to John Wesley (though it surely goes all the way back to the early church, and indeed to the Bible itself!). Wesley was convinced that Christians must be holy. I don't believe that every word of Wesley's teaching was perfectly scriptural. But much of it was. And more importantly, the motive behind his teaching was pure. He wanted to see Christian men and women act like Christian men and women. He wanted them to know the freedom of having complete victory over sin. He preached holiness, and he fathered an entire denomination, the Methodists, which held holiness as one of its central tenets. As is common in history, Wesley's descendants within the "holiness movement" drifted further and further from biblical truth, such that, a couple of generations ago, the holiness doctrine basically amounted to rules about skirt length and make-up and hair styles. (It still does in some increasingly narrowing circles.) The people of my generation (and many before) saw right through this silliness, and staged a mini-Reformation, swinging the pendulum firmly back to the side of "grace," where it has remained to this day.

But what is grace? The post-holiness grace proponents, in an effort to shun "legalism," have turned grace into a concept that is itself completely unbiblical. The grace message being preached today is: "It doesn't matter what you do, the Lord will forgive." And although this is true on some level, it is not true if by it you really mean, "You can go ahead and do whatever you want to do and get away with it, the Lord will forgive." This flippant attitude toward a holy God has led to apathy and complacency in our behavior. If we examine our lifestyles, it becomes obvious that the average "Christian" believes in his heart that he can basically live any way he wants, and it's ok, because he's already forgiven, or he can ask for forgiveness later. He may not answer that way out loud if you ask him, but his actions show that that is what is in his heart.

I used to be one of these. I remember reading through some of the "To-Don't Lists" in the New Testament, such as Galatians 5:19-21 or Ephesians 5:3-5, and thinking to myself, "I'm glad I'm saved so I don't have to worry about judgment for these kinds of acts." Duh! How stupid can you get?!? These people WILL NOT INHERIT THE KINGDOM OF GOD!

And let's not forget that Paul was writing this not to the unsaved but to the Church! Our skewed concept of grace has left us believing that a Christian is no more than a sinner who says some kind of a prayer akin to *abracadabra*, makes some sort of "intellectual assent to a set of scriptural propositions" (as Martyn Lloyd-Jones has phrased it), gets a free pass, then goes on doing the same things he used to do, but without fear of retribution. *The main idea of this book is that THAT IS NOT TRUE!*

Friend, we are called to holiness. And the fact that God requires it means He had to make a way to accomplish it. And He did! True grace, as one of my mentors often says, is unmerited favor AND divine enabling. Grace is not a free pass to behave poorly, it is divine power to overcome sin and live in freedom! Hallelujah!

My Journey in Holiness

It began with a simple, everyday reading of my Bible. I opened to Romans 8:1, and read:

> There is therefore now no condemnation to those who are in Christ Jesus, *who do not walk according to the flesh, but according to the Spirit.*

I was stunned. What was that little tag line (in italics)? I remembered having heard it before, but it had been many years. Nobody ever quotes it that way. And I had not read it that way for a long time, because the translations I had been reading left that line off. I thought to myself, "yeah, there's no condemnation, but only for those who walk according to the Spirit." I read the rest of the chapter. It seemed to be consistently speaking the same message. So much so that the little condition is repeated verbatim in verse 4. Christ fulfills "the righteous requirement of the law" in those:

> ...who do not walk according to the flesh but according to the Spirit.

So, even if this little condition wasn't in verse 1 in all of the manuscripts, it is in verse 4 in all the manuscripts, and it is equally Spirit-inspired, and it is the same message, in the same context.

I was pleased but cautious with my new revelation, since I had never really believed or been taught in that way. It took less than 24 hours for me to receive my first confirmation. The next day, I walked to the Jerry Falwell Library (next door to the building where I work), approached the bookcases, and chose, somewhat nonchalantly, a book to sit down with. The book just so happened to be a collection of sermons by John Wesley. I cracked the book in the middle, where it randomly opened to a sermon on none other than Romans 8:1! Needless to say, God had my attention. Sure enough, I found that Wesley read the passage the same way I had; the promise of *no condemnation* applies only to those "who do not walk according to the flesh, but according to the Spirit." The revelation God gave me on holiness had been confirmed.

As I began to reread the entire New Testament, with holiness in mind, I found it everywhere! I always knew it was there, but now, it was *really* there! I found that holiness is not just a component of Christian doctrine, it is a major component, an essential component.

More confirmations of my epiphany soon followed. About a month later, itinerant minister Josh Fontaine visited our church and preached a message that impacted our congregation profoundly. It was on "The Fuller's Field." God is calling us to the fuller's field to get clean. The message was a call to holiness. A month after that we began an 8-week series by John Bevere called "Killing Kryptonite." The message? Sin is the kryptonite that keeps us from moving in the power of the Spirit that is our inheritance as believers. In other words, it was a series on holiness.

My journey in understanding the necessity of holiness was paralleled (and still is!) by a journey of lifestyle. I can give testimony after testimony of sins and even sin-patterns in my life that I have overcome, one at a time, by the power of the Holy Spirit. Having conquered several, I am climbing the hill on more. Once those are conquered, I am quite sure the Lord will highlight another. This is sanctification. It is progressive. The key is not that I myself must overcome, but rather that my heart is postured to allow God to empower me. When sin is revealed in my life, I must turn from it. I cannot ignore the conviction and continue on in it. That is not the *modus operandi* of a true believer. A true believer says "yes" to the prompting of the Lord.

What to Expect in this Book

This book is one outcome of the journey I just described. I am going to take you through the entire New Testament, in just the same order that the Lord revealed it to me. First Romans 8, then Romans 6-7, then Romans 12-13, and the rest of the letter, followed by each of the other epistles, the Revelation, and closing with the Acts and the Gospels. I have mined each of the New Testament texts for any and all teachings they have on holiness. I'm limiting myself to the New Testament, since that seems to be where the break down in the modern evangelical mind is. We know God requires holiness in the Old Testament, but we somehow think He doesn't care about it anymore in the New. Or more precisely, we think He's "taken care of the requirement" by sending the Son. Yes and No. Yes the work is finished, but it's still on us to walk it out.

So that's it. An in-depth look at what the New Testament has to say about holiness. To be holy is to be set apart. That's what it means. We should look different from the world. We should be set apart. Now let me say that more plainly. Holiness is the practice of not sinning; and God has empowered true believers in Christ to overcome sin. This book lays out an overwhelming case that holiness is required of the New Covenant believer. And my hope is that God will work through this message to enlighten you, encourage you, embolden you, and empower you to live a sin-free life, the life that Jesus died to make possible for you!

One Last, Important Note

This book contains a LOT of Scripture. Now, I know that in most Christian books, it's easy to just gloss over the Scripture quotations and get on to the "point" the author is trying to make. I urge you strongly, don't do that with this book. This author is not trying to make any "points" apart from Scripture. I have carefully woven the Scripture into the text so that it actually reads as part of the thoughts I am expressing. In fact, all I am trying to do with this book is help you to see what the

Scripture is saying. It is so important that I would say, if you have to skip something, then skip the parts I have written and just read all the Scripture quotations in the order I have presented them, and let them speak to you. I can't emphasize this enough. You MUST carefully read every passage of Scripture quoted in this book as if it is embedded as part of the text itself, not as mere support to a point I'm making.

PROLOGUE:
HOLINESS IN THE OLD TESTAMENT

The majority of today's evangelical church believes holiness is optional and grace is sloppy. Even if we wouldn't admit we believe that, we prove it by our actions. One of the main reasons the church has veered off in this direction is because we have bought into the false notion that the God of the New Testament is different from the God of the Old Testament. The prevailing thought of the day is that God used to be harsh and judgmental and demanding, but now that Jesus has come and reconciled the world, He is instead forgiving and loving and merciful. But God did not shift from Righteous Judge to Merciful Savior, as if by quick costume change. He is and always has been and always will be both Righteous Judge and Merciful Savior. "For I am the LORD; I do not change" (Mal 3:6).

Not only has the LORD not changed, His plans for us have never changed. From the dawn of creation, He laid out a plan for us: *a duty, a calling, and a purpose.*

*Our **purpose** is and always has been to fellowship with Him.* To enjoy Him, to experience a relationship with Him, to share in the ecstasy of His nature. This is what the first family did as they walked with Him "in the cool of the day" (Gen 3:8). It's what we do when we "fellowship ... with the Father and with His Son Jesus Christ" (1Jo 1:3). And it is what we will one day realize fully, when we see Him "face to face" (1Co 13:12).

*Our **calling** is and always has been to reign with Him.* To use the authority that He delegated to us to influence, conquer, and rule in the earth. To live life as a holy adventure. This calling was articulated right from the beginning: "let them have dominion" (Gen 1:26). It is our promise for today, for He "is able to do exceedingly abundantly above all that we ask or think, according to the power that works in us" (Eph 3:20). And it is our final destiny: "they shall reign forever and ever" (Rev 22:5).

*Our **duty** is and always has been to fear Him and obey Him.* This was implied when God commanded, "of the tree of the knowledge of good and evil you shall not eat" (Gen 2:17). It is expressed concisely and directly in Ecclesiastes 12:13, "Fear God and keep His commandments: for this is the whole duty of man" (KJV). And it is a New Testament directive as well. "Love the Lord" is presented as the greatest commandment, and "this is the love of God, that we keep His commandments" (1Jo 5:3).

The Fall destroyed our ability to walk out our calling and fulfill our purpose. And although we were still technically able to do our duty of fearing Him and obeying Him (See Noah, Abraham, Job, etc.), that alone was not able to make us righteous, for "all have sinned" (Rom 3:23). A system of sacrificial offerings was put in place to "hold us over" until a permanent solution could manifest. That permanent solution,

Jesus, came to restore to us the ability to do our duty, live out our calling, and fulfill our purpose. *It is not at all that the requirements changed once Jesus came, it is rather that the requirements could actually be met once Jesus came!* The entire story of the New Testament is that God has made a way for us to be reconciled to Him, to reign with Him, and to have relationship with Him. I am convinced that the reason we are not experiencing greater levels of success in *our calling* and *our purpose* is that we have not submitted to Him fully in doing *our duty*. We do not fear God and keep His commandments. In other words, we have lost *holiness*.

* * * * *

Nevertheless, holiness is definitely a requirement, in the Old Testament, and in the New. Consider God's judgments in Genesis, first against Adam and Eve, then against Cain, then against the whole world by flood, then against Sodom and Gomorrah. All because they lacked holiness.

In Exodus, Moses had to take off his shoes in order to set foot on holy ground. In Leviticus, the nation of Israel offered sin offerings and guilt offerings. In Numbers, God sent poisonous snakes in judgment of the unholy Israelites. In Deuteronomy, the Lord laid out a litany of curses that He would put upon His own people if they did not obey Him (Ch. 28).

In Joshua, Israel lost the battle of Ai because of sin in the camp. In Judges, Samson's strength was taken because of his disobedience. In Ruth, the title character is described as a "virtuous woman" (3:11). In 1 Samuel, Saul's kingdom was taken from him because he was foolish and did not keep the

Lord's command. In 2 Samuel, David lost his son, the judgment of God upon his sin. In 1 Kings, the Lord tore the kingdom away from Solomon because he turned away from God and followed other gods. In 2 Kings, Gehazi was given leprosy in exchange for one greedy decision. In 1 Chronicles, the Lord struck down Uzzah in His righteous anger because of his irreverence in touching the ark. In 2 Chronicles, generations of idol worship finally caught up with Judah as they were conquered and exiled to Babylon. In Ezra, some of the returning exiles were unfaithful to the Lord by marrying foreign wives, and they were made to send their wives away and offer a ram for their guilt. In Nehemiah, the nation of Israel returned to God, confessed their sin, and took a vow of faithfulness; for this the Lord gave them joy (12:43). In Esther, the Lord sided with right over wrong, saving the Jews and turning the tables on the evil Haman.

In Job, the Lord allowed the accuser to attack Job, and when the test was passed, he was restored and his possessions were doubled. In the Psalms, we learn that the true sacrifice that is pleasing to God is a broken and contrite heart. In the Proverbs we learn that the pursuit of evil ends in death. In Ecclesiastes, we learn that fearing the Lord and keeping His commandments is the whole duty of man. In the Song of Solomon, the Shulamite is rewarded for her chastity.

In Isaiah, the prophet is undone when he realizes that he, too, is unclean. In Jeremiah, the prophet calls for Israel to repent of its apostasy. In Lamentations, Jerusalem cries out in agony because of the wages of her unholiness. In Ezekiel, the glory of the Lord departs from the temple because its inhabitants have defiled it. In Daniel, the repentant Nebuchadnezzar was

11

humbled and restored, but the unholy Belshazzar would not humble himself, and was destroyed. In Hosea, we see the depth of the Lord's mercy toward His adulterous people, and yet they still receive discipline because of their sin (10:9-10). In Joel, the Day of the Lord will bring judgment against all those who transgress the holy God. In Amos, God punishes Judah and Israel and anyone else who commits "crimes" against Him. In Obadiah, Edom's sins are met with judgment. In Jonah, God promised the utter destruction of Nineveh because of their unholiness. And when they repented, He relented. In Micah, Israel is judged for its rebellion. In Nahum, we learn that the Lord never allows the guilty to go unpunished. In Habakkuk, woe is pronounced against sinners with an assortment of sins. In Zephaniah, we are told to seek righteousness and humility so that we may be concealed in the day of the outpouring of God's wrath. In Haggai, whatever one who is defiled touches, that also becomes defiled. In Zechariah, God judges the enemies of Israel because of their detestable behavior. And in Malachi, God is a fire of judgment and purification, coming to restore holiness to His people and righteousness to their offerings.

Which brings us to the New Testament. Did God change? Did He simply decide that Jesus' death and resurrection "fixed" our problem once and for all, and now we can just act however we want because we're under a new covenant called *grace*? Does Jesus fulfill the requirement for holy living *instead of us*, or does He fulfill the requirement for holy living *through us*, if we allow Him to? Well, it's time to answer these questions. It's time to come to grips with the fact to which all of Scripture attests: *Holiness Is Not Optional.*

1
ROMANS 8

"Romans 8 has been called the most wonderful chapter in the Bible. It begins with 'no condemnation' and ends with 'no separation from God'." So writes one commentator.[1] True enough for those who are "in Christ Jesus." Unfortunately, many who believe they're living a life free of condemnation and free from separation, are actually living a life full of deception. Because they have not taken note of several conditions that are spelled out in between *no condemnation* and *no separation*. There is no condemnation and there is no separation:

1. If you do not walk according to the flesh, but according to the Spirit. (v. 4)
2. If the Spirit of God dwells in you. (vv. 9, 10, 11)
3. If by the Spirit you put to death the deeds of the body. (v. 13)
4. If you are led by the Spirit of God. (v. 14)
5. If you love God. (v. 28)
6. If God is for you. (v. 31)

We can't just take for granted that all six of these are true. This is literally a life-or-death issue. We'd better be sure we meet the qualifications for *no condemnation* and *no separation*. So, just for a moment, let's "examine ourselves" to see if we're in the faith (2Co 13:5). I would assume that most folks reading this book are believers, and many may be very sure of their salvation. Which is ok. We should be sure of our salvation if we're saved. But just for a minute, let's imagine we're not sure. Let's just visit hypothetical-land for a moment, and let Scripture give us an unbiased assessment of where we stand.

> There is therefore now no condemnation to those who are in Christ Jesus…
>
> -Romans 8:1a

Wonderful! Ok, what does it mean to be in Christ Jesus?

> … who do not walk according to the flesh but according to the Spirit.
>
> -Romans 8:1b (also, 8:4b)

Oh. To be in Christ Jesus means to walk according to the Spirit, and not according to the flesh. (Now *flesh* here does not mean muscles and skin. It means your carnal passions and appetites, the unholy desires that come from within your humanity, and not from God.) Ok, well what does it mean to walk according to the Spirit or to walk according to the flesh?

> For those who live according to the flesh set their minds on the things of the flesh, but those who live according to the Spirit, the things of the Spirit.
>
> -Romans 8:5

What is your mind set on? I'm going to ask that again. Take a moment to really reflect on the gravity of your answer. What is your mind set on?

Work backwards with me now. If your mind is set on the things of the flesh, then you are "walking according to the flesh." And if you are walking according to the flesh, then you are not "in Christ Jesus." And if you are not in Christ Jesus, then the promise of *no condemnation* does not apply to you! Oh God, have mercy on us!

Have we taken for granted that just because we raised our hand and walked down an aisle and said a little prayer one time years ago, that Romans 8 automatically applies to us? Is believing in Jesus merely some kind of mental assent to a truism, or is it a trusting faith that entails following Him in all things? "Even the demons believe—and tremble! But ... faith without works is dead" (Jms 2:19-20). Saving faith is not abstract and ethereal; it is trust enacted. It is *walking*.

Walking

Let's take a look at this little word *walk* for a minute. The opening of Romans 8 indicates that we can either walk according to the flesh or walk according to the Spirit. So what does it mean to walk? Walking is a continual repetition of putting one foot in front of another. It's a pattern. It's directional, it's goal-oriented. You don't walk nowhere, you walk somewhere. If you watched somebody take two steps forward, and two steps back, and two steps forward, and two steps back, and so on, you would not call that walking. You might call it rocking, or something else, but it would not be walking. The same would be true if someone took two steps forward and one step back, two steps forward and one step back, etc. That person would be moving forward, generally, but you would not call it walking. When you see walking, you know it's walking. It is steady, it is regular, it is smooth. If someone who is walking, stops and steps off the path for a moment to observe something, and then resumes walking, you say that that person is walking. A stop here and there does not constitute a change in the overall activity. It's a break in the pattern, but the pattern has been established, and the pattern is reestablished. Two steps forward and two steps back is a different pattern.

That's the way it is with walking according to the Spirit, and with walking according to the flesh. Which one is your pattern? Which is your default mode of operation? Do you take two steps in the Spirit, and then two steps in the flesh? If you sin, is it habitual? Are you walking according to the flesh? Or is it an occasional stumble, a break in your established pattern of walking according to the Spirit? If you sin, are you grieved by your sin, and do you then take that sin to the Lord in prayer and fervently call on Him to give you the strength and power to overcome? Or have you resigned yourself to sin as just a part of your life that you'll never be free from? Or do you even think about it at all?

Let's go beyond specific sins that we can put a name to. What is your general default attitude toward life? What is your mind set on? Maybe even things that are not sinful *per se*, but they are just things of this world. "Set your mind on things above, not on things on the earth" (Col 3:2). What is your mind set on? Certainly many hours of our day are spent at work or engaged in necessary tasks that are not particularly spiritual, and which require concentration. It is impossible to have our minds set on spiritual things 24/7. But when your task is complete, and your time is your own, *then where does your mind drift?* Do you drift to plans for the future? Your next purchase? Friends? Family? Social Media? Sports? Hobbies? Do you begin to worry? About anything and everything. Fear? Does your mind drift to a place where you've been hurt? Unforgiveness and bitterness? Do you spend your time thinking about how to find a girlfriend or a boyfriend or a husband or a wife? Are you contemplating all the problems in your marriage? All the problems at your job?

What is your mind set on? Those who live according to the flesh set their minds on the things of the flesh. And those who walk according to the flesh are not in Christ Jesus. And those who are not in Christ Jesus do not have a promise of *no condemnation.*

Well you might say that's tough talk. Yes it is. The Gospel is not a call to comfort, it's not a call to apathy, it's not a call to complacency, it's not a call to guilt-free self-centeredness. It's a call to total submission to the Lordship of Christ. The Gospel is the good news that Jesus has made a way for you to become righteous—*and to live righteously*—so that you can then fulfill your calling and purpose to reign with Him and to fellowship with Him. It's not a "good news" that says you get to do whatever you want without expecting judgment.

Take a Deep Breath

At this point you may be ready to put this book down. Please don't do that quite yet. Yes, this message is difficult. But it's the only way to eternal life. And if you stick with me a little longer—just one more chapter, in fact—you'll find out that the entire message, although difficult, is very encouraging. It is indeed *good news*! So sit back, take a deep breath, and let's look a little further into what Paul has to say in this chapter.

Three Laws

There's a little word in this passage that is critical for understanding the point being made. That little word is *law*. Now the word *law* has a couple of shades of meaning. On the one hand, it can mean "a standard to be attained or a rule to be followed." That's more of the formal meaning. Informally, it can be more of "a principle or impulse." Both meanings are found in this passage:

> For the *law* of the Spirit of life in Christ Jesus has made me free from the *law* of sin and death. For what the *law* could not do in that it was weak through the flesh, God did by sending His own Son in the likeness of sinful flesh, on account of sin: He condemned sin in the flesh, that the righteous requirement of the *law* might be fulfilled in us who do not walk according to the flesh but according to the Spirit.
>
> -Romans 8:2-4

The first two laws are principles or impulses. So, we can follow the principle or impulse of the Spirit, or we can follow the principle or impulse of sin and death. The third law, which is called simply *the law*, is referring to the Law of Moses, and thus implies the more formal *standard or rule* meaning. This is the same meaning intended by the fourth occurrence of the word *law* (v. 4). So, if I may paraphrase the passage, Paul is saying,

> If you follow the principle or impulse of God (which is another way of saying, if you walk according to the Spirit),

then the principle or impulse of sin and death is nullified in your life (which is another way of saying, there is now no condemnation toward you). Furthermore, this promise could not have been fulfilled by the Law (or standard) of Moses, because the weakness of our sin nature could never have allowed us to meet the requirements necessary for success under this system. Because "all have sinned" (Rom 3:23) and whoever stumbles in one point of the law is guilty of breaking it all (Jms 2:10). So what God did was to send His own Son, transfer the guilt of sin onto Him, and condemn Him. In so doing, the "righteous requirement" of the Law of Moses is fulfilled—by Jesus—in us—if we walk not according to the flesh but according to the Spirit. When we follow the principle or impulse of God, Jesus fulfills, in us, on our behalf, the requirement of the Law of Moses, which we are unable to fulfill on our own.

Led by the Spirit

So, to recap, if I follow the principle or impulse of God, which is to say, if I walk according to the Spirit, I can be assured that I have *no condemnation*, because Jesus will fulfill in me the righteous requirement of the Law of Moses. Then *how* exactly do I walk according to the Spirit?

> For those who live according to the flesh set their minds on the things of the flesh, but those who live according to the Spirit, the things of the Spirit.
>
> -Romans 8:5

I walk according to the Spirit by setting my mind on the things of the Spirit. Is it that simple? Yep. Do you have a problem with a particular variety of sin? Set your mind on the things of the Spirit. Commit every possible second you can to getting on your face before God and imploring Him to make the change in you.

Set your mind on Him. Set your mind on the solution, not the problem. See, we can't overcome sin by "trying harder." We can't overcome by our own power. We might succeed for a time, but eventually, we will always revert back. Only the Lord can make the change in you, from the inside out, that is necessary for complete deliverance from sin. Look to the Solution, not to the problem. Set your mind on Him. Cry out to Him in prayer. We're not talking about a 5-minute overture. The old saints used to talk about "praying through." Pray until you get the victory. Even if it takes years.

The unholy church is unholy because she is not serious about overcoming sin. Sin is not as repulsive to us as it is to God. We don't really care that it's there. It's not that important to us to get rid of it. If it's not important to you to get rid of it, you won't! You have to repent! That means "change your mind." You have to change your thinking. You have to allow Him to renew your mind, to give you a new mind that is not encumbered by that sin.

Only He can do it. Don't try to do it yourself. He does the work. You simply keep your eyes fixed on Him, earnestly calling on Him to do it, trusting that He will do it.

If we, instead, do not walk according to the Spirit, if we continue to keep our minds set on all of the distractions of the world around us, the prognosis is very bleak indeed:

For to be carnally minded is death...

-Romans 8:6a

For if you live according to the flesh, you will die...

-Romans 8:13a

20

The end of a life spent walking according to the flesh is death! Let that sink in. Perhaps you walked down an aisle, perhaps you knelt at an altar, perhaps you prayed the sinner's prayer. Then what? Did you get up from that place and turn around, turn from sin, do a complete 180? Did you stop walking according to the flesh and begin walking according to the Spirit?

No? Here's the good news: if you're reading this book, you're not dead, which means it's not too late! Start today! Turn around today! Fulfill your commitment to the Lord—the one you made, or the one you should have made. Don't just "accept Christ," but "receive Christ." Receive His power to overcome sin! If you will receive Jesus Christ by faith, and begin to walk according to the Spirit, then the promises of Romans 8 will be yours! No condemnation! No separation! Because:

> ... to be spiritually minded is life and peace. Because the carnal mind is enmity against God; for it is not subject to the law of God, nor indeed can be. So then, those who are in the flesh cannot please God. But you are not in the flesh but in the Spirit, if indeed the Spirit of God dwells in you. Now if anyone does not have the Spirit of Christ, he is not His. And if Christ is in you, the body is dead because of sin, but the Spirit is life because of righteousness. But if the Spirit of Him who raised Jesus from the dead dwells in you, He who raised Christ from the dead will also give life to your mortal bodies through His Spirit who dwells in you.
>
> Therefore, brethren, we are debtors—not to the flesh, to live according to the flesh. For if you live according to the flesh you will die; but if by the Spirit you put to death the deeds of the body, you will live. For as many as are led by the Spirit of God, these are the sons of God.
>
> -Romans 8:6b-14

To be led by the Spirit does not mean asking God whether you should buy cantaloupes or watermelons. At least that's not all it means. It means you allow the power of the Holy Spirit to empower you to live a life that is pleasing to Him, a life of overcoming sin! When we do that, we have assurance that we are "sons of God." And if we are sons, then we can cry out "Abba, Father" (Rom 8:15). Daddy! When we begin to fellowship with our Daddy, knowing that we are free, free from sin and free to pursue Him, then:

> The Spirit Himself bears witness with our spirit that we are children of God, and if children, then heirs—heirs of God and joint heirs with Christ...
>
> -Romans 8:16-17a

Hey! It's starting to sound a lot more like the "most wonderful chapter in the Bible" that it was billed as. And it is! But we can't forget that the reward is contingent on one very simple but sobering fact: we must "walk according to the Spirit."

Recapping the Conditionals

I opened the chapter with 6 conditional statements. We may now synthesize the overarching premise. If the Spirit of God dwells in you (vv. 9, 10, 11), then you will walk according to the Spirit and not according to the flesh (v. 4), by the Spirit you will put to death the deeds of the body (v. 13), you will be led by the Spirit of God (v. 14), you will love God (v. 28), and you can be assured that God is for you (v. 31). The end result of meeting these conditions is that we can expect (with no reservation, and with great anticipation!) *no condemnation* and *no separation* from God! What a wonderful chapter! Praise the Lord!

2
ROMANS 6

Part of me is sorry I opened with Romans 8. It likely gave you quite a jolt. There are many softer passages I could have eased into the subject with. But the other part of me is glad we've established the plumb line right off the bat. Romans 8:1, in the New King James Version, the version with the caveat—*to those who walk according to the Spirit*—was the verse that arrested me, and changed my thinking, giving me a new outlook on life. And now, it's up to you, whether you will join me in the pursuit of holiness, or whether you will be a hearer of the word only, and not a doer, observing yourself in the mirror only to walk away and forget what kind of man or woman you are (Jms 1:23-24). If you're ready to move forward, I have good news: in this chapter we find out that holiness is not just required, but is also, thankfully, *attainable*!

The "therefore" of Romans 8:1 refers backward to two thoughts, one from Chapters 1-5, and the other from Chapters 6-7. Reaching back to Chapter 5, Paul had made the claim that:

...through one man's [Adam's] offense judgment came to all men, resulting in condemnation, even so through one Man's [Jesus'] righteous act, the free gift came to all men, resulting in justification of life.

-Romans 5:18

Without Jesus there is condemnation. With Jesus there is no condemnation. This is the thought that Paul resumes in Romans 8:1. But before he can continue his main idea, he feels strongly that he needs to take some time to make sure we don't get the wrong idea. Because the staggering truth of the Gospel is that:

...where sin abounded, grace abounded much more.

-Romans 5:20

This is such an audacious claim that Paul is nervous that some of the baby Christians may get the idea that sinning is now an acceptable practice, because it's covered by the blood. Sound familiar? He asks a rhetorical question, a question which, if anyone were indiscreet enough to ask in earnest, would expose a truly vile and disgusting motivation:

Shall we continue in sin that grace may abound?

-Romans 6:1b

The answer Paul provides to his own question takes up the next two chapters of Scripture. The short answer given in verse 2, a resounding NO!, is not complete enough. He is adamant—inspired by the very Spirit of God—that we get this right. So, let's take a long hard look.

What shall we say then? Shall we continue in sin that grace may abound? Certainly not! How shall we who died to sin live any longer in it? Or do you not know that as many of us as were baptized into Christ Jesus were baptized into His death? Therefore we were buried with Him through baptism into death, that just as Christ was raised from the dead by the glory of the Father, even so we also should walk in newness of life.

-Romans 6:1-4

How could we possibly live in sin? We died to sin. The reason a life of sin is impossible is because we were baptized into death. That means that when Jesus died, we died, too. But not only has our old man died, our new man lives with a "newness of life."

Here is where we run into a problem in today's church. The average Christian understands she has been *buried* with Christ, but she does not understand she has been *raised* with Christ to *newness* of life. We believe that the death of Christ has erased the guilt of our sin, providing for us the "not guilty" verdict we call *justification*. But we do not believe that, by being raised with Christ, we have also the responsibility (and the power!) to walk sin-free. But we do! Paul explains further:

For if we have been united together in the likeness of His death, certainly we also shall be in the likeness of His resurrection, knowing this, that our old man was crucified with Him, that the body of sin might be done away with, that we should no longer be slaves of sin. For he who has died has been freed from sin.

-Romans 6:5-7

What does it mean to be freed from sin? John Wesley spoke of sin as having three distinct aspects, which he called the *guilt* of sin, the *power* of sin, and the *being* of sin.[2] The **guilt** of sin refers to the fact that anyone who transgresses a holy God (which is every single human being) is judged to be guilty of a heinous infraction, and will be sentenced to death (Rom 6:23). The **power** of sin refers to the fact that, as fallen humanity, sin is victorious over us, it is our master and we are its slaves. Apart from Christ, it is impossible for us, even those sinners who live a relatively moral life and do good works, to escape the gravity of sin's power over us. We cannot, on our own, overcome the power of sin that forces us into the positional identity of "sinner." The **being** of sin roughly corresponds to what some refer to as the sin nature. There is a difference between the sins that I commit and the sin that I am *in*, that I am born into. Another way to think about the being of sin is that it is the *capacity to sin*. There is a sin-factory within us; and that sin-factory only knows how to produce sin.

So, (unsaved) sinners carry the guilt of sin, meaning their sin results in condemnation; they are subject to the power of sin, meaning that they can't not sin no matter how hard they try (which doesn't mean they have to commit every single variety of sin, but rather, there is at least one sin-type that they will not be able to refrain from under their own power); and they possess the being of sin, meaning that the capacity to sin is innate within them, and even if they did not commit individual sins, they would still have an inescapable propensity toward sin.

So, what does it mean to be freed from sin? *Jesus freed us from two of the three aspects of sin.* We who have been united with Christ in death and resurrection have been freed from the *guilt* of sin and the *power* of sin, but not the *being* of sin. The guilt of sin is erased by His substitutionary atonement; we have now been given a "not guilty" verdict. AND, the power of sin has been abrogated; we are no longer slaves to sin, and we have been given power, by the Holy Spirit, to overcome sin. But the *being* of sin remains. Even though I now walk guilt-free, and have the power to not-sin, the capacity to sin remains within me. This never goes away. I will always continue to have a choice to make, whether I will exercise my God-given power to overcome sin, or whether I will instead yield to the *being* of sin, that sin-factory within me that can produce sin, if I allow it.

> Now if we died with Christ, we believe that we shall also live with Him, knowing that Christ, having been raised from the dead, dies no more. Death no longer has dominion over Him. For the death that He died, He died to sin once for all; but the life that He lives, He lives to God. Likewise you also, reckon yourselves to be dead indeed to sin, but alive to God in Christ Jesus our Lord.
>
> -Romans 6:8-11

Reckon yourselves. That word *reckon* is borrowed from the world of accounting. You might think of it in terms of balancing a checkbook. There is a certain amount in your checking account, and that won't change, even if you believe there's a different amount. Let's say you have $800 in your checking account, but you think you have $400. The way you are "walking" is consistent with having $400, but you actually have $800. You need to *reckon* your checking account. You need to operate in a manner consistent with what is actually *the case*. And so it is with sin and the work of Jesus. If you are in Christ, you are dead to sin and alive to God. This is the actual state of affairs of your bank account. Thus, you should operate in a manner consistent with that truth. You should *reckon* yourself to be dead to sin and alive to God, because being dead to sin and alive to God is the actual state of affairs. In other words, if you are in Christ, you are dead to sin; START ACTING LIKE IT!

> Therefore do not let sin reign in your mortal body, that you should obey it in its lusts. And do not present your members as instruments of unrighteousness to sin, but present yourselves to God as being alive from the dead, and your members as instruments of righteousness to God.
> -Romans 6:12-13

Let's remember this word *present.* It comes back later, and we'll want to make the connection when it does. We present ourselves to God. Some other translations read "offer." See, God does all the work, He works through us to overcome sin. We simply present ourselves to Him, offer ourselves to Him, trusting that He will do it. We don't "try harder," we rather set our minds on Him, more intentionally, more frequently, and more intensely.

> For sin shall not have dominion over you, for you are not under law but under grace.
> -Romans 6:14

And here it is, folks! The moment you've all been waiting for. This is the verse that once-and-for-all settles the issue of the power of sin. Not only are we free from the guilt of sin, we are free from the power of sin. SIN DOES NOT HAVE DOMINION OVER YOU! Reckon yourself to that fact. Jesus did not die a horrible death so that you could walk down an aisle, accept a proposition, and walk away unchanged. He died so that you could have POWER OVER SIN! So that you could live a life that is sin-free! I believe this with all of my heart: at the moment of conversion, the Holy Spirit comes to take up residence in the human heart to empower you, so that, hypothetically, it is possible for you to never sin again!!! This is why John writes, "*If* anyone sins" (1Jo 2:1). Because it's not a foregone conclusion that we will! We don't have to anymore! Because sin no longer has dominion over us! We have dominion over it!

This is the message of encouragement! Yes, walking according to the Spirit, living the Christian life, is not easy. But it is possible. It is possible to walk in victory. Victory over worry, victory over fear, victory over unforgiveness, victory over addiction, victory over sexual sin, victory over sinful thoughts, victory over sinful actions. Holiness is attainable! Sin does not have dominion over us! If indeed we are His. Would you rather take the easy way out in this life, do your own thing, go on sinning, go on setting your mind on the things of the flesh, and end in death? Or would you rather commit yourself fully to God, present yourself to Him to do the work of sanctification in your life, walk according to the Spirit, use the power of God to overcome sin, and live? He sets before you a choice. Choose life!

What then? Shall we sin because we are not under law but under grace? Certainly not! Do you not know that to whom you present yourselves slaves to obey, you are that one's slaves whom you obey, whether of sin leading to death, or of obedience leading to righteousness? But God be thanked that though you were slaves of sin, yet you obeyed from the heart that form of doctrine to which you were delivered. And having been set free from sin, you became slaves of righteousness. I speak in human terms because of the weakness of your flesh. For just as you presented your members as slaves of uncleanness, and of lawlessness leading to more lawlessness, so now present your members as slaves of righteousness for holiness.

-Romans 6:15-19

Here we see, officially for the first time, the theme of *holiness* emerge explicitly. We've been reading about "walking according to the Spirit" and "reckoning ourselves dead to sin." Now we have a name for all that: *holiness*. We used to present ourselves, we used to offer ourselves as slaves of sin, but now we are to present ourselves as slaves of righteousness, so that we can attain holiness, so that we can reckon ourselves dead to sin, so that we can walk according to the Spirit.

For when you were slaves of sin, you were free in regard to righteousness. What fruit did you have then in the things of which you are now ashamed? For the end of those things *is* death. But now having been set free from sin, and having become slaves of God, you have your fruit to holiness, and the end, everlasting life.

-Romans 6:20-22

Let's take note of a new word here: *fruit*. We will make more of it in the next chapter when it returns. When you were a slave of sin, there was fruit that came out of that experience, and it wasn't good fruit. And had you continued in that (or, if you continue in that) the result would have been death. But now—notice the progression—you are a slave of God, which results in fruit called holiness, and the end of all that (other translations read "the result" of all that) is everlasting life! How does one attain everlasting life? Belief? Yes, but what kind of belief? We believe in the Lord Jesus Christ as our only means of salvation, to cleanse us from the guilt of sin, and to empower us to overcome sin. We then begin to walk according to the Spirit, we establish a pattern in our lives of sin-free living. If we do sin, we repent. The pattern of sin-free living may be broken for a moment, but sinful living does not itself become the pattern. As slaves of God, we do what He says when He says it, for that is what it means for Him to be our Lord. In so doing, we begin to bear fruit, which is holiness. AND THE END OF ALL THAT IS EVERLASTING LIFE!

> For the wages of sin is death, but the gift of God is eternal life in Christ Jesus our Lord.
>
> -Romans 6:23

Don't miss the context of this verse. The gift of God is eternal life in Christ Jesus our Lord. What kind of gift is this? The gift is eternal life, which, as we have seen, is made possible by the two sub-gifts of "freedom from the guilt of sin" and "freedom from the power of sin." The gift of eternal life is "the end" of the gift of "empowerment to live a life free from sin, bearing fruit, becoming holy."

This eternal life, according to Romans 6:23, is "in Christ Jesus our Lord." *Christ*, meaning *Anointed One*, refers to the Messiah, the One who would be anointed (with oil) King. *Jesus* means *Savior*, and His name stands for all that is associated with the salvific acts: substitutionary atonement, justification, and so on. *Lord* is another way of saying *Master*. It is specifically denoting the Master-slave relationship, and specifically referring us back to the "slaves to God" motif Paul has just been explaining in Chapter 6.

Christ the King, you the subject; Jesus the Savior, you the sinner-turned-saint; Lord the Master, you the slave—you can't have one without the others, you must be "in Christ Jesus our Lord" to receive the gift of eternal life.

3
ROMANS 7

Beginning in Romans 7, Paul begins to change the flavor of the discussion a bit. He is still aimed at defending the necessity of holiness, which is the fruit of a life devoted to walking according to the Spirit. But now he adds to the discussion a second layer, which is the concept of "the law." He wants to make sure that we understand that the Law of Moses cannot make us holy. And in fact, it was never designed to do so. Instead, the Law was put in place to make us aware that we are sinful. And Paul explains the Law using a fascinating analogy to a man and wife:

> Or do you not know, brethren (for I speak to those who know the law), that the law has dominion over a man as long as he lives? For the woman who has a husband is bound by the law to her husband as long as he lives. But if the husband dies, she is released from the law of her husband. So then if, while her husband lives, she marries another man, she will be called an adulteress; but if her

husband dies, she is free from that law, so that she is no
adulteress, though she has married another man. Therefore,
my brethren, you also have become dead to the law
through the body of Christ, that you may be married to
another—to Him who was raised from the dead, that we
should bear fruit to God.

-Romans 7:1-4

Paul likens us to a woman who is married to a husband that
she does not want, which is the Law. She wants her husband to
die so that she can marry another, much more desirable man,
Jesus. But instead of the man dying, it is in fact the woman (us)
who dies. Because we died, our marriage to the Law is null and
void, and we are now free to marry the more desirable
bridegroom, Jesus.

Now notice the purpose of this marriage at the end of verse
4: "that we should bear fruit to God." Well, this analogy should
be plain enough to comprehend. The bride of Christ is married
to the groom, Christ, for the purpose of bearing fruit. Clearly,
"bearing fruit," in this metaphor, refers to *having children*. The
very first command of God to the first couple, "Be fruitful"
(Gen 1:28), has never been retracted. Except, like so many
biblical concepts, what was physical in the Old is now spiritual
in the New. We do not bear physical human children to Christ;
rather we, collectively, bear to our Bridegroom, spiritual
offspring. And that offspring, that fruit, was already defined five
verses earlier: "your fruit" is *holiness* (Rom 6:22). And this fruit of
holiness, we are to bear "to God." So, let's step back for a
moment and get the whole picture.

> For when we were in the flesh, the sinful passions which were aroused by the law were at work in our members to bear fruit to death.
>
> -Romans 7:5

That is, when we were married to the Law, we produced sinful spiritual offspring.

> But now we have been delivered from the law, having died to what we were held by, so that we should serve in the newness of the Spirit and not in the oldness of the letter.
>
> -Romans 7:6

In so doing, we, the bride of Christ, now produce the spiritual offspring of holiness unto God. God sent His Son to be our Savior, so that He could then be our Lord, so that He could then be our Bridegroom, so that we could then produce the spiritual offspring of holiness. Oh, Church! Of how much more benefit could we be to the kingdom if, instead of just hoping to get to heaven on the fastest and most comfortable train, we were of the mindset that we do not want to leave this earth until we have done what He desires for us to do—to bear the fruit of holiness to God?!

The Battle for Holiness

In verses 7-13 Paul again answers a hypothetical question. If the Law produced sin and death in me, does that make the Law bad? Of course he says "no." Rather, the Law is good, indeed the standard of goodness, and it stands before me as a measuring stick showing that I have not met its requirements. The contrast between the Law and the human lawbreaker is then made plain:

For we know that the law is spiritual, but I am carnal, sold under sin.

-Romans 7:14

Now when Paul says he is carnal, he is not saying that he consistently gives into his carnal desires. He is not confessing that he walks according to the flesh. He is saying, the sin-factory still exists within me. I still have the capacity to sin. (John Wesley would say "I still have the *being* of sin.") There is something inside me that is bent toward sin, which is what we call *the flesh*, and that flesh, those carnal appetites, never go away. But—this is the key—they are defeated by the cross! The flesh has to follow the way of sin, but the flesh no longer has legitimate power in my life. Thus I am free and empowered to walk according to the Spirit, and to refuse to obey the commands that sin gives the flesh.

Then Paul describes how hard this actually is to do by making a bit of a confession:

For what I am doing, I do not understand. For what I will to do, that I do not practice; but what I hate, that I do. If, then, I do what I will not to do, I agree with the law that it is good. But now it is no longer I who do it, but sin that dwells in me. For I know that in me (that is, in my flesh) nothing good dwells; for to will is present with me, but how to perform what is good I do not find. For the good that I will to do, I do not do; but the evil I will not to do, that I practice. Now if I do what I will not to do, it is no longer I who do it, but sin that dwells in me.

-Romans 7:15-20

That's quite a mouthful. Simplifying drastically, the sin-factory within Paul wants to do evil, whereas the new-creation-Paul wants to do good. And therein lies a constant battle. And he actually confesses to doing wrong. But—and this is a very important point—I am convinced that the sins Paul confesses here are not of the same types that he preaches against in nearly all of his letters. There's no way he's involved in sexual sin, or drunkenness, or lewdness, or wrath; none of the giant sins. No, he is surely referring primarily to his thought-life, perhaps an occasional action. Perhaps he has the thought once in a while to take it easy and become too complacent. Perhaps he did not use quite enough grace when speaking to someone he didn't particularly enjoy talking to. Perhaps he thinks too highly of himself from time to time. I know I would if I were him. I mean, after all, he is the man!

But then he recognizes, "Hey! This is an unholy thought! I shouldn't be thinking this! Oh, God, my flesh is at it again! Please flood me again to overpower this flesh and get me to the place where I only think thoughts that are pleasing to you." I'm convinced that most of the sins Paul might confess to, many of us wouldn't even consider to be sinful. But they cause him holy grief, because he absolutely hates hurting the heart of God.

Now he returns to the different laws, specifically the ones that are of the type "principles or impulses."

> I find then a law *[principle or impulse of sin]*, that evil is present within me, the one who wills to do good. For I delight in the law of God according to the inward man. But I see another law in my members, warring against the law of my mind *[principle or impulse of God]*, and bringing me into captivity to the law of sin which is in my members. O wretched man that I am! Who will deliver me from this body of death? I thank God—through Jesus Christ our

Lord. So then, with the mind I myself serve the law of God, but with the flesh the law of sin.

-Romans 7:21-25

Now again, he's not saying that he does a lot of sinning but that it's ok because of grace. He's simply saying that the sin-factory is always present, and we must constantly be on guard, with our minds set on the things of Spirit, so that we do not yield to the sin-factory.

The very next verse is Romans 8:1. We have seen that the "no condemnation" motif refers back to Romans 5:18. But now we can also see that the "therefore" does indeed refer back to the aside of chapters 6-7 as well.

There is therefore now no condemnation to those who are in Christ Jesus, who do not walk according to the flesh, but according to the Spirit.

-Romans 8:1

There are two competing forces within me: the Holy Spirit and the sin-factory. Once in a while, the sin-factory may get the better of me, but it doesn't have to, because sin has no dominion over me. If the pattern of my life, my *modus operandi*, my default setting, my *walk*, is "according to the Spirit," I can expect no condemnation. If I do sin, I repent, call out to the Lord to cleanse me of my sin and empower me to overcome the next time I am tempted. With a firm assurance of salvation, I don't beat myself up, but rather focus fully on Him, trusting Him to do the work in my heart, never giving up the fight until He has secured the victory in me.

4
ROMANS 12-13

Romans 6-8 is the passage in which we learn that holiness is not inconsequential, it is not unattainable, and it is not optional. Romans 12-13 is the passage in which we actually, *therefore*, receive the explicit call to holiness, as well as some specifics of what that should look like. In between is another *aside* (Romans 9-11), this one dealing with the nature of Israel. So when Paul returns to his main idea at the beginning of Chapter 12, he is saying, "Given everything I said about holiness in Chapters 6-8, I am urging you in the strongest possible way: 'BE HOLY!'"

> I beseech you therefore, brethren, by the mercies of God, that you present your bodies a living sacrifice, holy and acceptable to God, which is your reasonable service.
> -Romans 12:1

When we understand the depth of what God has done for us, it is reasonable, it is the least we can do, to be holy. You see the direct connection back to chapter 6 found in the word *present*.

He was saying there, you used to present yourself as a slave to sin, but now you should present yourself as a slave to obedience. He then showed that the end of all that was eternal life, no condemnation, relationship with Abba Father, and no separation from God! And so he picks it back up here, "Therefore! Please, please, please, be holy! That way you can actually walk in these promises that are available to you."

> And do not be conformed to this world, but be transformed by the renewing of your mind, that you may prove what is that good and acceptable and perfect will of God.
>
> -Romans 12:2

This is holiness: not being conformed to the world. Are you conformed to the world? Does your life basically look just like any non-Christian we could pick out of a line-up? Do you watch TV just as much as your secular neighbor? Do you scroll social media just as much as your secular neighbor? Do you spend money on essentially the same stuff as your secular neighbor? Do you spend time on yourself about as much as your secular neighbor? What do you think it might look like to not be conformed to the world?

But be transformed. I find it interesting how certain things are phrased in Scripture. On whom does the onus fall? Some things fall to God to take care of. Justification, reconciliation, sanctification, just to name a few. But being transformed seems to fall to us, at least on some level. It doesn't say, "He will transform you by renewing your mind." It says "be transformed." There's a piece of this that we have to take ownership of. I have to choose to allow the Lord to transform me. I have to choose to allow Him to renew my mind. He won't force His way on me in this.

To-Do Lists and To-Don't Lists

Most of the next three chapters of Romans lay out some specifics of what a life of holiness should look like. Paul spent the first eight chapters explaining why it's necessary; now he spends the rest of the letter telling us what it actually entails. He begins with a to-do list:

Let love be without hypocrisy. Abhor what is evil. Cling to what is good. Be kindly affectionate to one another with brotherly love, in honor giving preference to one another; not lagging in diligence, fervent in spirit, serving the Lord; rejoicing in hope, patient in tribulation, continuing steadfastly in prayer; distributing to the needs of the saints, given to hospitality.

Bless those who persecute you; bless and do not curse. Rejoice with those who rejoice, and weep with those who weep. Be of the same mind toward one another. Do not set your mind on high things, but associate with the humble. Do not be wise in your own opinion.

Repay no one evil for evil. Have regard for good things in the sight of all men. If it is possible, as much as depends on you, live peaceably with all men. Beloved, do not avenge yourselves, but rather give place to wrath; for it is written, "Vengeance is Mine, I will repay," says the Lord. Therefore, "If your enemy is hungry, feed him; If he is thirsty, give him a drink; For in so doing your will heap coals of fire on his head." Do not be overcome by evil, but overcome evil with good.

Let every soul be subject to the governing authorities. For there is no authority except from God, and the authorities that exist are appointed by God. Therefore whoever resists the authority resists the ordinance of God, and those who resist will bring judgment on themselves. For rulers are not a terror to good works, but to evil. Do you want to be unafraid of the authority? Do what is good, and you will have praise from the same. For he is God's minister to you for good. But if you do evil, be afraid; for he does not bear the sword in vain; for he is God's minister, an avenger to execute wrath on him who practices evil. Therefore you must be subject, not only because of wrath but also for conscience' sake. For because of this you also pay taxes, for they are God's ministers attending continually to this very thing. Render therefore to all their due: taxes to whom taxes are due, customs to whom customs, fear to whom fear, honor to whom honor.

Owe no one anything except to love one another, for he who loves another has fulfilled the law. For the commandments, "You shall not commit adultery," "You shall not murder," "You shall not steal," "You shall not bear false witness," "You shall not covet," and if there is any other commandment, are all summed up in this saying, namely, "You shall love your neighbor as yourself." Love does no harm to a neighbor; therefore love is the fulfillment of the law.

-Romans 12:9-13:10

Wow! There's a lot to do to fulfill the call to holiness. Love, service, patience, steadfastness in prayer, taking care of others' needs, living peaceably, submitting to authority. And we're just getting started! When Paul says to present yourself as a slave to God, in holiness, when he says to walk according to the Spirit so that you will receive no condemnation, these are the specific kinds of things he is referring to.

Then he includes a short *to-don't list* at the end of Chapter 13.

Let us walk properly, as in the day, not in revelry and drunkenness, not in lewdness and lust, not in strife and envy. But put on the Lord Jesus Christ, and make no provision for the flesh, to fulfill its lusts.

-Romans 13:13-14

Revelry, drunkenness, lewdness, lust, strife, envy. Let's make sure we understand the nature of these forbidden acts. Revelry and drunkenness go together. Revelry is the behavior resulting from drunken parties in which folks get out of control, make a public spectacle of themselves, and perhaps even riot. Lewdness and lust go together as well. Lewdness refers to sexual intercourse outside the bond of marriage, and lust refers to sexual excess or a lack of sexual restraint that is shameless and willful and reveals a lack of regard for what is right. Strife and envy go together as well. Strife is a bitter conflict or discord, and envy denotes, in addition to jealousy, fierce indignation or zeal in defending something.[3]

After forbidding these six sins, Paul then says we are to "make no provision for the flesh, to fulfill its lusts." It's one thing to say you want to be holy, to say you want to stop sinning, to say you want to be free from addiction. But it's quite another thing to "make no provision for the flesh." You want to quit pornography? What steps have you taken to ensure that pornography has no provision? Have you removed the internet from your phone? Have you moved your computer from a private location to a public one? If you live with another person, do you make a point of not being home alone? If you live by yourself, are you trying to find a roommate? Do you have an accountability partner? One who will truly hold you accountable? How badly do you really want to be free?

Now this is just one example. But the principle applies to anything: make no provision for the flesh.

Now I must clarify something here. Taking preemptive steps to block temptation is not the same thing as becoming sanctified from the inside out. We might liken the former to a steroid, and the latter to an antibiotic. When you are sick, you may be prescribed a steroid to ease some of the symptoms, but that will eventually be worthless if you do not also take the antibiotic, which actually kills the disease. Jesus is the antibiotic; making no provision for the flesh is the steroid. The idea is to do everything you can to keep that temptation away (steroid) until the Lord completes His work in you (antibiotic). So, make no provision for the flesh. But at the same time, set your mind on the things above. Regularly gazing on God, including regular intake of the Word of God, will cleanse you, in time.

5
ROMANS

At this point, we've covered enough ground to be able to zoom out and see the big picture on Paul's letter to the Romans. The "main idea" of the letter comprises five sections: 1:16-3:20, 3:21-3:31, Chapter 5, Chapter 8, and 12:1-15:13. Before and after these sections—in 1:1-1:15 and 15:14-16:27—we find an exordium and a postscript, respectively. The remaining sections, Chapter 4, Chapters 6-7, and Chapters 9-11, serve as asides, in which the main idea is elucidated or supported in some way.

So what is the main idea? Let's take it section by section, and then I'll summarize it. In section 1, Paul makes the point that the problem with the world is *unrighteousness*, which includes things like:

> ... sexual immorality, wickedness, covetousness, maliciousness ... envy, murder, strife, deceit, evilmindedness;
> -Romans 1:29

Sinful people are:

backbiters, haters of God, violent, proud, boasters, inventors of evil things, disobedient to parents, undiscerning, untrustworthy, unloving, unforgiving, unmerciful;

-Romans 1:30-31

Then Paul makes a startling statement. He writes that some of us—remember this letter is addressed to the Church—are passing judgment against these people, and yet doing the same things. We can't point the finger at them, and not also point it back at ourselves. Because apart from grace, "there is no one righteous" (Rom 3:10). And notice how strong the language is:

> Do you really think—any of you who judges those who do such things yet do the same—that you will escape God's judgment? Or do you despise the riches of His kindness, restraint, and patience, not recognizing that God's kindness is intended to lead you to repentance? Because of your hardened and unrepentant heart you are storing up wrath for yourself in the day of wrath, when God's righteous judgment is revealed.
>
> -Romans 2:3-5 (CSB)

Now don't miss this:

> He will repay each one according to his works: eternal life to those who by persistence in doing good seek glory, honor, and immortality; but wrath and anger to those who are self-seeking and disobey the truth while obeying unrighteousness.
>
> -Romans 2:6-8 (CSB)

First of all note that he cannot be offering eternal life to a person who keeps the Law, since (1) No one has ever kept the whole Law, and (2) He would have had to say "He *would* repay." God *would* repay someone with eternal life who was able to keep the whole Law. But He won't, because no one can. But this says, "He *will* repay each one according to his works." It doesn't say "according to your *faith*," it says "according to your *works*." You ask, "Are you saying we're saved by works?!" No, I'm saying (because Paul is saying) the only kind of faith that results in eternal life is the kind of faith that is evidenced by works! Look at the kinds of words Paul uses to clarify the point: "persistence in doing good." We are NOT repaid eternal life by merely believing **that** Jesus died for us. We are repaid eternal life by believing **in** Jesus to forgive us AND empower us to "persist in doing good!"

The Structure of Romans

Exordium	1:1-1:15
Section 1	**1:16-3:20**
Section 2	**3:21-3:31**
Aside	Chapter 4
Section 3	**Chapter 5**
Aside	Chapters 6-7
Section 4	**Chapter 8**
Aside	Chapters 9-11
Section 5	**12:1-15:13**
Postscript	15:14-16:24

Having established that no one is righteous, neither the Jew nor the Gentile, Paul unpacks God's solution to this problem in the second section of the main idea.

> But now the **righteousness** of God apart from the law is revealed ... through faith in Jesus Christ, to all and on all who believe ... being **justified** freely by His grace through the **redemption** that is in Christ Jesus, whom God set forth as a **propitiation** by His blood, through faith ...
>
> -Romans 3:21-25

To really understand the solution to the problem of 1:16-3:20, read 3:21-25 in reverse; the solution is: *Jesus Christ as propitiation, leading to redemption, leading to justification, leading to righteousness.* Now, in case you're not familiar with those terms, let me give brief explanations. Jesus was sent as *propitiation*, meaning His substitutionary sacrifice appeased or placated or satisfied the righteous judgment and holiness of God. Because of this propitiation, we were *redeemed*, which means we were released to freedom by the payment of a ransom. The propitiation also secured our *justification*, which is our "not guilty" verdict. This is the piece we've been referring to when we said that Jesus died to free us from the guilt of sin. And because we are redeemed and justified, we are made *righteous*, which is to say we are in right-standing with God.

The Problem

1:16-3:20	Unrighteousness

The Solution

3:21-3:31	Propitiation, Redemption, Justification, Righteousness ...
Chapter 5	Peace, Reconciliation, Salvation ...
Chapter 8	No Condemnation *IF* ...
12:1-15:13	Holiness

Paul makes quite a big deal of the fact that this is all accomplished "by grace, though faith." And he wants to drive this point home, which he does in the aside of Chapter 4, in which he shows that Abraham, even before the law, was justified by faith.

Having completed the aside, he returns, at the beginning of Chapter 5, to the main idea—section three of the main idea, if you're keeping track. And he picks right up on the sequence he established at the end of Chapter 3: propitiation, redemption, justification, righteousness …

> Therefore, having been justified by faith, we have **peace** with God through our Lord Jesus Christ,
>
> -Romans 5:1

And …

> Much more then, having now been justified by His blood, we shall be saved from wrath through Him. For if when we were enemies we were **reconciled** to God through the death of His Son, much more, having been reconciled, we shall be **saved** by His life.
>
> -Romans 5:9-10

The next three steps in the solution are peace, reconciliation, and salvation. *Peace* meaning tranquility and assurance of salvation with freedom from fear; *reconciliation* meaning restoration to favor; and *salvation* meaning rescued from perishing and restored to health. And note that salvation is the only one so far that is phrased in the future tense: we shall be saved. This doesn't mean that we aren't saved now. We have been saved (2Ti 1:9), we are being saved (1Co 1:18), we are saved (Eph 2:8), and we will be saved (Rom 5:10). But part of the equation is "will be." It's not all done until it's done. Part of being saved is walking it out, persevering to the end, persisting in doing good (Rom 2:6).

The next connection in the main idea (Section 4) is that because of the propitiation, redemption, justification, righteousness, peace, reconciliation, and salvation we have through faith in Christ; we have *no condemnation*, provided that we walk according to the Spirit and not according to the flesh. The condemnation brought on by Adam is nullified by Christ. This connection between Romans 5:18 and Romans 8:1 is interrupted by the aside of Romans 6-7, in which Paul takes great pains in ensuring that we don't get the idea that we should go on sinning. And he puts the exclamation point on this doctrine by writing that:

> ... having been set free from sin, and having become salves of God, you have your fruit to holiness, and the end, everlasting life.
>
> -Romans 6:22

And ...

> For if you live according to the flesh you will die; but if by the Spirit you put to death the deeds of the body, you will live.
>
> -Romans 8:13

After the final aside of Chapters 9-11, it only remains for Paul to make the call to holiness explicit, which he does in section five of the main idea (Rom 12:1-15:13). "Given everything I have just said about how eternal life is the end result of a life of holiness, patterned after the things of the Spirit, I implore you to be holy! It's the only way!" Such is the message of the apostle.

The Real Roman Road

One of the cute little evangelistic tricks popular in Christian circles is the so-called Roman Road. This is a splicing together of several verses that generate a framework for "getting saved." It has several variations, but usually always includes at least the four following verses:

> For all have sinned and fall short of the glory of God.
> -Romans 3:23

> For the wages of sin is death, but the gift of God is eternal life in Christ Jesus our Lord.
> -Romans 6:23

> But God demonstrates His own love toward us, in that while we were still sinners, Christ died for us.
> -Romans 5:8

> That if you confess with your mouth the Lord Jesus and believe in your heart that God has raised Him from the dead, you will be saved.
> -Romans 9:10

While I don't doubt that these four verses provide a path to salvation, in light of our journey thus far, I think we would have to say that these are probably not the best verses to use for such an explanation. In fact, three of the four—the first, the second, and the fourth verse—are totally out of place. Let me explain.

"For all have sinned and fall short of the glory of God" is the negative in the middle of possibly the most positive passage of all Scripture. Romans 3:21-26 is the solution(!)—"but God..."—not the problem. So stating the problem using this verse is a little strange. In place of Romans 3:23, let's consider Romans 3:10, which states essentially the same idea, and does so within an entire passage that communicates the same idea: no one is righteous.

Next, Romans 6:23 is also taken out of context if it is cherry picked for evangelistic purposes. First of all, the Roman Road makes it seem as if 6:23 is a challenge to sinners to be saints. But we now know better; it is in fact buried in a passage, specifically directed to the Church, in which holiness is the idea in mind. Paul is saying in Chapter 6, "If you've been saved, you cannot go on sinning, because you are dead to sin (vv. 1-2). If you instead do what you're supposed to do, which is to live holy, the end of that will be eternal life (v. 22). Let's make it more plain: sin ends in death, but God has given eternal life to those who overcome the power of sin by His Spirit (v. 23)." That's not a message of evangelism directed at sinners, that's a message of sanctification directed at saints! If we wish to communicate the message that "the wages of sin is death," we could do so as effectively using 1:18, which states that the wrath of God will be poured out on all unrighteousness. This verse, and not 6:23, is found in the context of a challenge to sinners that they'd better get right, or else.

Now Romans 5:8, on the other hand, does actually work pretty well. It lets us know Jesus' death is the catalyst for all of the blessing promised by "the Gospel." But even that one, without a pretty deep background in theology (which the typical unchurched sinner does not have, of course), can give the wrong impression. When we say that God demonstrates His love, we can easily get the impression that God loved us "soooooooo much." That's the way we like to read John 3:16. But John 3:16 doesn't mean that. The CSB translates it correctly:

For God loved the world *in this way*: He gave ...
-John 3:16a (CSB)

God didn't love us sooooo much. He loved us *so*, He loved us *in this particular way*: He gave. He wasn't Grandpa-in-the-sky; we were His enemies!!! He gave His Son in spite of being in direct opposition to us. For this reason, Romans 5:6 might be a better option. It still indicates that Christ died for us. And, an added bonus, as you will see, it starts with "For" instead of "But," which will make for a better flow once we put this all together.

Finally, Romans 9:10. There are several issues here. The first is that this verse comes from an aside about the nature of Israel. It is really not a part of the letter's main idea. That doesn't mean we can't use it, it just means it's cherry picked. We can do better.

The larger issue with Romans 9:10 is that, by itself without context, it gives the impression that salvation is a *magic-wand proposition*. "Confess with your mouth" and "believe in your heart." How hard can that be? Pretty hard actually. How many have walked down the aisle at a Billy Graham crusade to confess with their mouths and believe in their hearts? What are they confessing and believing? Confessing that Jesus is Lord? We can confess it, but if we don't actually submit to Him as slave to Master, we will be the ones in Matthew 7:21 who merely say "Lord, Lord" but are not known by Him. And believing in our hearts that God raised Him from the dead? Even the demons believe *that*. To be saved, we must believe *in*. We must put our trust in the impartation of the power of Jesus' resurrection to give us newness of life!

It's important that when we present the Gospel to people, we let them know what they are really signing up for. The Gospel is this: I used to be evil, but God made a way for me to be good. The Gospel is NOT this: I used to be evil, but God made a way for me to keep being evil and get away with it. So instead of Romans 9:10, I would suggest that Romans 3:22 gives us the correct notion, in context, that salvation is to "all who believe." And then Romans 8:1 and 8:13 help us to understand what that believing looks like. (And if you're not using KJV or NKJV, I would also add 8:4 so that we make sure we get the piece we've made such a big deal about: "who do not walk according to the flesh, but according to the Spirit.")

Putting it all together now, let's consider this the new-and-improved Roman Road. Perhaps not comprehensive, but enough to give any person drawn by the Spirit unto God the language to understand what a commitment to Christ entails:

For the wrath of God is revealed from heaven against all ungodliness and unrighteousness of men ...
-Romans 1:18a

As it is written: There is none righteous, no, not one
-Romans 3:10

But now the righteousness of God apart from the law is revealed ... through faith in Jesus Christ, to all and on all who believe ...
-Romans 3:21-22

For when we were still without strength, in due time Christ died for the ungodly.

-Romans 5:6

There is therefore now no condemnation to those who are in Christ Jesus, who do not walk according to the flesh, but according to the Spirit.

-Romans 8:1

For if you live according to the flesh you will die, but if by the Spirit you put to death the deeds of the flesh, you will live.

-Romans 8:13

6
CORINTHIANS

If the churches of the New Testament were Paul's "class," then the church at Corinth would definitely be the worst student in the class. The Corinthian church was the most immature and the most sinful of all the churches that Paul addressed. Paul talks about holiness in his two epistles to the Corinthians, probably more so than any other of his letters, precisely because many of them were not being holy. Knowing this should help us as we turn now from the theology of Romans to the practical instruction of First and Second Corinthians.

1 *Corinthians 3*

Apparently there was a fairly significant dispute among the Corinthians regarding whom they should look to as a leader. Some looked to Paul, others to Peter, others to Apollos (1:12). And Paul's first objective in this letter was to repair these "divisions" that manifested as a result of "envy" and "strife" (3:3). And he says something very interesting about these issues:

And I, brethren, could not speak to you as to spiritual people but as to carnal, as to babes in Christ. I fed you with milk and not with solid food; for until now you were not able to receive it, and even now you are still not able; for you are still carnal. For where there are envy, strife, and divisions among you, are you not carnal and behaving like mere men? For when one says, "I am of Paul," and another, "I am of Apollos," are you not carnal?

-1 Corinthians 3:1-4

Why do I say that this statement is interesting? For two reasons. First, Paul notes that it is carnal—or we might say, walking according to the flesh—to operate in envy, strife, and division. My what a high bar! It's not just the biggies, it's not just the adultery and fornication and murders and thefts that are off limits. No, we can yield to our carnal appetites, our flesh, by merely allowing divisions to come between us and our fellow believers. If we are truly Spirit-people, we cannot and will not allow petty differences to divide us. Differences are ok, divisions are not. How many so-called believers today will not fellowship with each other because one says "I am of Calvin" and another says "I am of Arminius?" Or "I am of Methodism" and "I am of Presbyterianism." Or "I am of contemporary worship music" and "I am of traditional church music." Are you not carnal?! Are you not walking according to the flesh to allow such nonsense to keep the fellowship broken?

Second, apparently *there is such a thing as a carnal Christian!* This seems to fly in the face of our discussion of Romans. In particular, given what we said about Romans 6-8, such a statement seems like it would be an impossibility: those who walk according to the flesh are *not* "in Christ Jesus." But here, it seems that the Corinthians are both "in Christ Jesus" (1:2) *and*

57

"carnal" (3:4)! How can this be? Well at this point I must merely offer my own personal opinion on the matter. This is simply what seems right to me. I believe that a person can accept Christ, and yet be immature and even carnal in their faith, operating in many ways out of ignorance. They don't "get it," at least not completely. They may even read the Scriptures, and many passages may blow right past them. For whatever reason, the content, the truth of those passages does not "land" in their spirits and take root. Their lifestyles may even look quite a bit like the world. Maybe I'm even talking to you. You "accepted Christ" once upon a time, but you are not following Him whole-heartedly. You have no prayer life, your church attendance is sporadic, your giving is minimal, your television or smartphone is your god, sports and entertainment rule your life, you are offended by the least little thing, you are not gracious toward people, you basically do your own thing and do not put others first, etc. Ok, so you ask me, "Then how do I know whether I am a carnal Christian or I am just deceived and not a Christian at all?" And my response would be: if you're truly a Christian, when you realize the error of your ways, when you see the light, when you feel that conviction in your heart, when you "get it," then you will be faithful to turn from those things that you have been doing wrong, and begin to follow the Lord as best you can in the things you know to do. That's how a carnal Christian graduates to a sanctified Christian. If, on the other hand, you are reading these words, and you feel something inside you that pushes back and says "No, I don't want to live that way. I want to keep doing what I'm doing. I want to live my life the way I want to live it. I don't want to be holy. Or, it would be nice to be holy but it's really not worth it. It's not a requirement, and

I'm not going to submit myself to a standard that tough because I really don't think I have to. I can make it to heaven without it." I beg to differ! When you are confronted with your sin, and you really understand that what you're doing is sinful, if you refuse to turn from it, then you are in rebellion, you are not a Christian, the promises of God in Christ are not yours, and you are in a very undesirable position indeed.

Paul is pointing out the sin in this church in hopes—indeed, I believe with the expectation—that they will turn from it. If they do, they show themselves to be the Christians Paul knew all along that they were. If they don't, they show by their actions that they are not His.

1 Corinthians 5

This is made even clearer in the next portion of the letter. Having addressed the question of divisions sufficiently, Paul turns, in Chapters 5-6, to a much more heinous problem: sexual immorality.

> It is actually reported that there is sexual immorality among you, and such sexual immorality as is not even named among the Gentiles—that a man has his father's wife! And you are puffed up, and have not rather mourned, that he who has done this deed might be taken away from among you. For I indeed, as absent in body but present in spirit, have already judged (as though I were present) him who has so done this deed. In the name of our Lord Jesus Christ, when you are gathered together, along with my spirit, with the power of our Lord Jesus Christ, deliver such a one to Satan for the destruction of the flesh, that his spirit may be saved in the day of the Lord Jesus. Your glorying is not good. Do you not know that a little leaven

leavens the whole lump? Therefore purge out the old leaven.

-1 Corinthians 5:1-7a

First of all, it should be clear from these two passages that there are "levels" of sin. For the sin of divisions addressed in Chapter 3, Paul simply tells them to stop doing it. For the sin of a man having his father's wife addressed in Chapter 5, Paul tells them to excommunicate him. I do not buy the notion, put forward by some, that sin is sin and it's all the same. It is the same in the sense that any sin, no matter how small or big, separates us from God and requires the atonement of Christ. But all sins are not created equal. This does not mean that we should not be grieved upon the commission of low-level sins, but it does mean that there are certain sins that the Lord corrects "in stride," and others for which there is zero tolerance. You cannot "accept Christ," and then go on for the next three years murdering people, praying that the Lord will help you overcome that sin "in time" as part of your sanctification process. There are certain sins that are a putrid stench, an abomination before a holy God. And the Church is given instruction in Scripture, to deal with these harshly. But we are not doing it in today's Christendom. We smooth things over and look past, and we coddle and say, "It'll be ok." No it won't! If you are engaged in adultery or fornication, including pornography(!), and you are confronted by your Christian brothers and sisters, and you still do not repent, do not change, do not turn from your sins; if you refuse to "put to death the deeds of the body by the Spirit" (Rom 8:13), you are not fit for communion with the Body of Christ, and you should be released from the Church.

But that's not the end of the story. When we "deliver such a one to Satan," it's not a judgment upon their soul (that's not our job), it is rather a last-ditch effort to help that person see the error of his ways and the gravity of his plight. When the church looks at a man and says, "Your sinful lifestyle is not worthy of continued fellowship with God and His people," it is a time for that man to come to himself and see the light. The hope is always for restoration. We hope that such a person will indeed turn fully to the Lord. And this is what Paul hoped for the man in 1 Corinthians 5, but he wasn't willing to let him spoil the whole loaf of bread with his leaven in the meantime.

Then Paul clarifies the point:

> I wrote to you in my epistle not to keep company with sexually immoral people. Yet I certainly did not mean with the sexually immoral people of this world, or with the covetous, or extortioners, or idolaters, since then you would need to go out of the world. But now I have written to you not to keep company with anyone named a brother, who is sexually immoral, or covetous, or an idolater, or a reviler, or a drunkard, or an extortioner—not even to eat with such a person.
>
> For what have I to do with judging those also who are outside? Do you not judge those who are inside? But those who are outside God judges. Therefore "put away from yourselves the evil person."
>
> -1 Corinthians 5:9-12

We see here that this is actually the second letter Paul has written, since he notes in verse 9 that he had already written them not to associate with sexually immoral people. This is a big deal! He is now addressing it in two separate letters. "Do not keep company with sexually immoral people."

But he draws a distinction between those who call themselves Christians and those who do not. We are allowed to associate with sinners of all kinds who do not claim Jesus as Lord. How else will they be drawn to Him? That doesn't mean we develop close friendships with worldly people, and consequently allow ourselves to be enticed away from the Lord. (This point is in fact stated explicitly later in the letter: "Do not be deceived: 'Evil company corrupts bad habits'" (1Co 15:33).) But it does mean that we do not avoid sinners out of some self-righteous motive. But we *do* avoid those who are living in sin while claiming the name of Jesus. We are not even to eat with them! And not just sexually immoral people, but the covetous, idolaters, drunkards, extortioners, and revilers (which means people who speak abusively and disgracefully).

And notice the nuance in the types of judgment implied here. We do not get to judge sinners (in the world) at all. Nor do we get to judge whether or not someone is a "Christian" and will be rewarded with eternal life; only Jesus can do that, in the last day. But we do get to judge whether a church member is acting like a Christian, and what kind of discipline that behavior merits, even to the extent of excommunication.

Now, we must be careful here. All of this must be done in grace, and with the compassion that longs for the ultimate restoration of the individual. At no point should we revel in tossing people out of our church. We can certainly think of certain sects of Christianity which have abused this passage, turning it into license to wield unholy power and fear over congregations. That is not the idea at all, and I rather think that sort of thing would be tolerated in the eyes of God about as much or less than these heinous sins themselves.

1 Corinthians 6

Paul shifts the focus of his rebuke slightly at the beginning of Chapter 6, only to return to it at the end of the chapter. He refers to an incident in the church in which disputes between brethren have led to law suits. And he sort of echoes Jesus' call to "love your enemies" as he really drills down to an essential pillar of Christianity:

> Why do you not rather accept wrong? Why do you not rather let yourselves be cheated?
>
> -1 Corinthians 6:7b

At no point in the Christian walk do we get to put ourselves first. We always defer to others, sometimes at great cost to ourselves.

Then he gives us another to-don't list, this one longer than the one in Romans:

> Do you not know that the unrighteous will not inherit the kingdom of God? Do not be deceived. Neither fornicators, nor idolaters, nor adulterers, nor homosexuals, nor sodomites, nor thieves, nor covetous, nor drunkards, nor revilers, nor extortioners will inherit the kingdom of God.
>
> -1 Corinthians 6:9-10

Paul really covers the bases on the sexual sins here. He wants to leave no wiggle room. *Fornicators* refers to unmarried people engaged in sexual behavior. *Adulterers* refers to married people engaged in unlawful sexual behavior, outside the bond of the marriage. *Homosexuals* refers to male-male sexual behavior, particularly where one is underage. And *Sodomites* refers to sexual intercourse between two males, or between two females. It's all sin, and none of it is allowed. Such people "will not inherit the kingdom of God!"

But that's not all. Besides those in sexual sin, idolaters, thieves, covetous, drunkards, revilers, and extortioners; these, too, will not inherit the kingdom of God.

Paul closes this section with one final proscription against sexual sin. And he begins to give us a reason why we shouldn't be doing it:

> Flee sexual immorality. Every sin that a man does is outside the body, but he who commits sexual immorality sins against his own body. Or do you not know that your body is the temple of the Holy Spirit who is in you, whom you have from God, and you are not your own? For you were bought at a price; therefore glorify God in your body and in your spirit, which are God's.
>
> -1 Corinthians 6:18-20

Your body is the temple of the Holy Spirit. When you commit sexual sin, you are desecrating the temple of the living God! This should not be so! And furthermore, you were redeemed, "bought at a price." You are a slave; you don't get to do what you want, you have to do what He says. "Therefore glorify God in your body and in your spirit!"

1 Corinthians 10

As much counsel against sin as Paul has given so far, he is not done yet. He makes one more drag of the net in Chapter 10, in which an even more grave warning is issued.

> Moreover, brethren, I do not want you to be unaware that all our fathers were under the cloud, all passed through

the sea, all were baptized into Moses in the cloud and in the sea, all ate the same spiritual food, and all drank the same spiritual drink. For they drank of that spiritual Rock that followed them, and that Rock was Christ. But with most of them God was not well pleased, for their bodies were scattered in the wilderness.

Now these things became our examples, to the intent that we should not lust after evil things as they also lusted. And do not become idolaters as were some of them. As it is written, "The people sat down to eat and drink, and rose up to play." Nor let us commit sexual immorality, as some of them did, and in one day twenty-three thousand fell; nor let us tempt Christ, as some of them also tempted, and were destroyed by serpents; nor complain, as some of them complained, and were destroyed by the destroyer. Now all these things happened to them as examples, and they were written for our admonition, upon whom the end of the ages have come.

-1 Corinthians 10:1-11

Wait a minute! I thought this was the New Covenant! What is this about the judgment of death?! Did he just say that the Israelites in the wilderness are "examples" we are to use for admonition, teaching us how we should act today, and what we can expect if we don't? Yep. They all "ate the same spiritual food" and "drank the same spiritual drink." And yet many complained, and worse, descended into idolatry and sexual immorality. And for this God responded with a judgment of death. Don't miss this! Paul is talking to THE CHURCH, not to unbelievers. And he says, "Hey, everybody here has tasted of the same spiritual food and drink; everybody has heard the Gospel and come to the knowledge of Jesus, and familiarity with the Holy Spirit. Don't do what the Israelites did, and ignore this revelation, and go on sinning. If you do, you will meet the same judgment they did!" Whoa!!!

Ladies and gentlemen, this is not a game we're playing. God is very serious. And He is holy. And He will not abide an unholy people. Yes, He is Father, and yes He is good, and yes He is merciful. But He is the righteous Judge, and there will be a judgment day, and if you're not holy, you will be judged accordingly, because you have not actually received the protection of the blood of Jesus because you have not received His empowering grace to overcome sin.

But we can overcome! And Paul closes this warning by encouraging us to do so:

> Therefore let him who thinks he stands take heed lest he fall. No temptation has overtaken you except such as is common to man; but God is faithful, who will not allow you to be tempted beyond what you are able, but with the temptation will also make the way of escape, that you may be able to bear it.
>
> -1 Corinthians 10:12-13

Keep on guard. Don't get the idea that just because you're doing well now means you'll always do well. And take heart, because there is nothing that you can't overcome! God will not allow you to be tempted beyond what you are able to overcome. He *is* a good Father! He has made a way of escape. So don't get discouraged and operate in a defeated mindset that says that you can't do it. You *can* do it, by the Spirit. You must have the Spirit to do it. Anyone who totally surrenders to the Lordship of Christ is empowered to overcome any sin!

2 Corinthians

The theme of holiness is peppered throughout the second epistle, though it is not presented nearly as forcefully or prominently as it is in the first. Paul addresses the necessity of forgiveness in Chapter 2, the "new creation" in which all things are made new in Chapter 5, and the need to refrain from being unequally yoked with unbelievers in Chapter 6. "Therefore," he writes as Chapter 7 opens:

> ... having these promises, beloved, let us cleanse ourselves from all filthiness of the flesh and spirit, perfecting holiness in the fear of God.
>
> -2 Corinthians 7:1

He then commends them for actually doing what he told them to do in the previous letter. And he clarifies his own motives in asking them to do it.

> For even if I made you sorry with my letter, I do not regret it; though I did regret it. For I perceive that the same epistle made you sorry, though only for a while. Now I rejoice, not that you were made sorry, but that your sorrow led to repentance. For you were made sorry in a godly manner, that you may suffer loss from us in nothing. For godly sorrow produces repentance leading to salvation, not to be regretted; but the sorrow of the world produces death. For observe this very thing, that you sorrowed in a godly manner: What diligence it produced in you, what clearing of yourselves, what indignation, what fear, what vehement desire, what zeal, what vindication! In all things you proved yourselves to be clear in this matter.
>
> -2 Corinthians 7:8-11

He didn't like having to be so firm, but it was necessary to produce the repentance. It was a godly sorrow that they felt, which produced "repentance leading to salvation." Let this sink in. We don't simply walk down an aisle and "get saved." We walk out a life of holiness, repenting when necessary, and this life well lived *leads to salvation*! "Are you saying I haven't been saved?" you ask. Not exactly. You were saved, you are being saved, and you will be saved; IF you walk not according to the flesh but according to the Spirit. The work of Christ is finished: justification, sanctification, and glorification. It *was* done; justification. It *is being* done; sanctification. And it *will be* done; glorification. It is ALL *by Him*, but it only applies if we walk it out.

In the back half of the letter, Paul indicates in a few different ways, that he is nervous about returning to Corinth. He is hoping that when he does, he will find that there really has been true repentance, and total repentance. And he gives some pretty stiff warnings, in the event he arrives and finds that that is not the case.

> For I fear lest, when I come, I shall not find you such as I wish, and that I shall be found by you such as you do not wish; lest there be contentions, jealousies, outbursts of wrath, selfish ambitions, backbitings, whisperings, conceits, tumults; lest, when I come again, my God will humble me among you, and I shall mourn for many who have sinned before and have not repented of the uncleanness, fornication, and lewdness which they have practices. This will be the third time I am coming to you. "By the mouth of two or three witnesses every word shall be established." I have told you before, and foretell as if I were present the second time, and now being absent I write to those who

have sinned before, and to all the rest, that if I come again I will not spare—

-2 Corinthians 12:20-13:2

In other words, "You better shape up before I get there, or I will be unsheathing my sword and laying you all out on the floor." Paul is not playful when it comes to sin, and he is not nonchalant when it comes to professing Christians living a "my way" lifestyle. Instead, he writes:

Examine yourselves as to whether you are in the faith. Test yourselves. Do you not know yourselves, that Jesus Christ is in you?—unless indeed you are disqualified.

-2 Corinthians 13:5

There is a philosophy floating around Christian circles today that idolizes the "assurance of salvation." Paul had no such philosophy. He was very clear and very consistent in his writings. Your assurance of salvation is not based on some abstract, ethereal concept that you have come into agreement with. If you are not living right, you should examine yourself to see whether you are in the faith. Is it possible that you are "disqualified"?

7
GALATIANS

Let's take some time now to address this concept of *legalism*. Surely at this point, many readers—if they've made it this far—are bothered by the emphasis that I am putting on what we *do* as believers. You may be saying, isn't that legalism? Isn't that works-based salvation? Doesn't "salvation by faith" mean that I don't have to *do* anything, except believe? Well, no, actually it doesn't mean that. Salvation by faith means that I put my trust in the finished work of Christ (that is, I "believe in Jesus") to cleanse me from the guilt of past sins and to empower me to overcome present and future temptation of sin. And to answer the first two questions: no, we are not talking about legalism, and no, we are not talking about works-based salvation.

The idea of *legalism*, which I am basically equating with *works-based salvation*, says that there is something good in me that effects (in other words, it is efficacious in bringing about) my own salvation. Legalism says "following the law (rules) saves me." Works-based salvation says "doing good things saves me."

All of this line of thinking is heresy. Only Jesus saves. Jesus is the only Way to the Father (Jhn 14:6). But if you believe in Jesus and confess Him as Lord, He will produce the fruit of holiness in you, by His Spirit. If you do not see the fruit of holiness growing in you as you live out the Christian life *after believing*, you should, as Paul writes, "Examine yourself" to see if you are actually in the faith at all.

Here are some helpful ways to understand the difference between legalism and holiness. First understand that the difference is a question of cause and effect. Legalism says, "be*cause* I do good things and follow all the rules, the *effect* is that I am saved." Holiness says, "be*cause* I have been saved, purchased by God, to become His slave, the *effect* is that I turn away from the practice of sinning and begin to walk according to the Spirit." Legalism says, "If you do this and don't do that, you will earn a position." Holiness says, "If you have been given a position, then you will do this and not do that."

Then, understand that a lifestyle of holiness is not about *trying* to live right. Legalism says "try, try, try" to be holy. Holiness says "trust, trust, trust" that He will make you holy. When I sin, I don't sit around and beat myself up over it. I grieve that I have grieved the Lord, but I do not go back and replay it in my mind in order to condemn myself. I don't dwell on it at all. I don't set my mind on the things of the flesh. I turn my attention to Him. I get on my face and cry out to the Lord to take that unholiness from me, to empower me not to do that particular thing again, to clear away that predisposition to act or think in that unholy way. I don't "try" to beat the sin myself. I "trust" that He will beat it for me. But—and this is a very important but—I don't excuse the sin either, and I don't assume that I will always be plagued by such-and-such disposition. I know the sin-factory will remain in me until my dying day, but I do not consider it a foregone conclusion that the particular sins I may be prone to will always be a problem for me. I fully believe He will defeat them. I can't say enough about the battle-plan of keeping your focus on the Lord, and not on the sin.

The Counterpoint of Legalism and Holiness in Galatians

It's important to understand the difference between legalism and holiness, and it's particularly important as we turn now to the epistle to the Galatians. Why? Because the primary message of Galatians is: *do not fall for legalism.* And yet in the middle of this warning against legalism, Paul makes one of his strongest calls for a commitment to holiness!

The Message of Galatians

To understand the impact of the counterpoint of the holiness message, let's set the stage by getting a feel for the main message to the Galatians, which was not holiness, but rather *freedom from the Law.*

> I am amazed that you are so quickly turning away from him who called you by the grace of Christ and are turning to a different gospel—not that there is another gospel, but there are some who are troubling you and want to distort the gospel of Christ.
>
> -Galatians 1:6-7 (CSB)

Paul goes on to specify that the "different gospel" he is referring to is the gospel of the Judaizers, those who have come in to the ranks of these new Christians and told them that, in addition to believing in Christ, they should also keep the Law of Moses, and in particular the rite of circumcision. (Remember from our discussion of Romans that Jesus fulfills the Law of Moses in us who follow the Law of God, that is, in us who walk according to the Spirit.) Paul recounts his own testimony, showing that he, in fact, is a pretty important Jew himself, and he has also had a revelation from God, and he knows what he's talking about. And even Titus, who is a Gentile, was not "compelled to be circumcised" (2:3). He sort of puts an exclamation point on the theological side of his argument by stating:

> For if I build again those things which I destroyed, I make myself a transgressor. I do not set aside the grace of God; for if righteousness comes through the law, then Christ died in vain.
>
> -Galatians 2:18, 21

So intense is his righteous indignation against these troublemaking heretics that he even says that he wished they would castrate themselves (5:12)! And within this address, well over four chapters in length, Paul makes this important statement regarding the relationship of justification and sanctification:

> O foolish Galatians! Who has bewitched you that you should not obey the truth, before whose eyes Jesus Christ was clearly portrayed among you as crucified? This only I want to learn from you: Did you receive the Spirit by the works of the law, or by the hearing of faith? Are you so foolish? Having begun in the Spirit, are you now being made perfect by the flesh?
>
> -Galatians 3:1-3

The Galatians were justified by faith, not by the works of the Law. They will likewise be sanctified by faith, and not by the works of the Law. But notice this phrase, "works of the Law." Every time Paul uses the word *works* in Galatians to refer to working our way into the kingdom, he uses the phrase "works of the Law," never just *works* by itself. What's my point? Good works, born of faith, the evidence of faith that James so clearly pointed to (Jms 2:14-24), are not at all what Paul is referring to here. "Works of the Law" are in no way necessary, but the "works of holiness" are necessary.

Holiness: The Counterpoint to the Message of Galatians

How do I know there is a distinction between the "works of the Law" and the "works of sanctification"? How do I know that there is a difference between legalism and holiness? Because right here in the middle of this diatribe against legalism, Paul makes it very clear that living a life of holiness is still the expectation:

> For you, brethren, have been called to liberty; *only do not use liberty as an opportunity for the flesh,*
>
> -Galatians 5:13a

Take a moment to let that sink in. You are free. Free from what? Free from the Law. But don't get the idea that your freedom should be stretched to the point where you think you're free from carrying out the basic duty of mankind, to fear God and keep His commandments. "Do not use liberty as an opportunity for the flesh."

...but through love serve one another. For all the law is fulfilled in one word, even in this: "You shall love your neighbor as yourself." But if you bite and devour one another, beware lest you be consumed by one another!

I say then: Walk in the Spirit, and you shall not fulfill the lust of the flesh. For the flesh lusts against the Spirit, and the Spirit against the flesh; and these are contrary to one another, so that you do not do the things that you wish. But if you are led by the Spirit, you are not under the law.

-Galatians 5:13b-18

Don't miss this:

Now the works of the flesh are evident, which are: adultery, fornication, uncleanness, lewdness, idolatry, sorcery, hatred, contentions, jealousies, outbursts of wrath, selfish ambitions, dissensions, heresies, envy, murders, drunkenness, revelries, and the like; of which I tell you beforehand, just as I also told you in time past, that those who practice such things will not inherit the kingdom of God.

-Galatians 5:19-21

Will not inherit the kingdom of God! He is writing to the Church! He's not preaching an evangelistic message and telling sinners to turn from their sin. He is writing to believers, and he is saying, "you cannot do these things, because if you do, you will not inherit the kingdom of God." Justification does not exist in isolation! If one is justified, one will also be sanctified. In fact, if one is justified, one will also have redemption, righteousness, peace, reconciliation, salvation, sanctification, and no condemnation. (See our discussion of Romans.) The multi-faceted work of God is a "package deal." One does not simply "believe," and then sit around for 40 years and wait on a trip to heaven. We believe, we repent, and we follow! Period.

Having laid out yet another *to-don't list* in verses 19-21, Paul then articulates probably the most complete and most significant of all of his to-do lists in verses 22-23, the list we refer to as the fruit of the Spirit.

> But the fruit of the Spirit is love, joy, peace, longsuffering, kindness, goodness, faithfulness, gentleness, self-control. Against such there is no law. And those who are Christ's have crucified the flesh with its passions and desires. If we live in the Spirit, let us also walk in the Spirit.
>
> -Galatians 5:22-25

Now we already know from Romans 6:22 that the fruit that we bear to God is holiness. What we get here is a more detailed description of what that holiness will look like. These nine characteristics make up what holiness is. The fruit of the Spirit is holiness. And these are the expressions and characteristics of what the fruit of holiness entails: love, joy, peace, longsuffering, kindness, goodness, faithfulness, gentleness, self-control.

8

EPHESIANS

The letter to the Ephesians naturally breaks into two parts, the first (Chapters 1-3) primarily doctrinal in its focus, and the second (Chapters 4-6) primarily practical in its focus. This is important because when we get down to the nuts and bolts of what we're supposed to be doing—that is, the practical part—it can be summed up in one word: holiness. But even before the practical half, several principles of holiness doctrine are expressed in the first half of the letter.

Why We Were Chosen

The significance of holiness is established right off the bat. Paul tells us that God "chose us in Him before the foundation of the world," and that the reason is "that we should be holy" (1:4). Wow. God created us, called us, marked us, why? Because He wanted a people that was holy. He never had any intention of simply looking over a crowd of sinners and pronouncing some guilty and some not-guilty. For the sake of what? No, He came, He died, to secure a holy people. To truly rescue mankind from sin—both the guilt of sin and the power of sin—so that we could be pleasing to Him.

By Grace Through Faith ... For Works

For good reason, the Church, post-Reformation, has made much of the little phrase, "by grace through faith." This is the way of salvation. We are saved by grace through faith. No other way. We can't earn it. It's a gift. It is only received through faith, and it is only given by grace. The key verses on this doctrine are found in Ephesians 2:

> For by grace you have been saved through faith, and that not of yourselves; it is the gift of God, not of works, lest anyone should boast.
>
> -Ephesians 2:8-9

Very clear. Cut and dried. And nothing in this book should be taken—intentionally or unintentionally—as a denial of this truth!

However. It is eye-opening to read around these verses, to see them in the context of the entire passage. We find, when we do so, that the truth of "by grace through faith" does not contradict the requirement of holiness. First, note the implication of the first four verses:

> And He made you alive, who were dead in trespasses and sins, in which you once walked according to the course of this world, according to the prince of the power of the air, the spirit who now works in the sons of disobedience, among whom also we all once conducted ourselves in the lusts of our flesh, fulfilling the desires of the flesh and of

the mind, and were by nature children of wrath, just as the others. But God ...

-Ephesians 2:1-4a

You "once walked according to the course of this world." We "once conducted ourselves in the lusts of our flesh, fulfilling the desires of the flesh and of the mind." Is this not obvious? We once lived this way. "Once" means we shouldn't be living that way anymore! It's past tense. We walked, we conducted, we fulfilled. Not anymore! "By grace through faith" in verse 8 is designed to ensure that the way we "once" lived is not the way we live any longer! In case you need further proof, verse 10 makes it explicit.

not of works, lest anyone should boast. For we are His workmanship, created in Christ Jesus for good works, which God prepared beforehand that we should walk in them.

-Ephesians 2:9-10

I included verse 9 so you could see the connection from the "works" that don't save us to the "works" that "God prepared beforehand that we should walk in." We still have to do works! We are His work, and He made us to do works. The works don't save us. They are not the cause, they are the effect. But they *are* the effect! You can't just not do works. If you are saved, you will do good works.

More Walking

Having laid out some pretty robust doctrine in the first three chapters, Paul turns, in the fourth, to more practical matters. Given everything he has explained about God and His relationship to man, how should we then conduct ourselves? Paul's answer, once again, is *walking*.

> I, therefore, the prisoner of the Lord, beseech you to walk worthy of the calling with which you were called,
>
> -Ephesians 4:1

Now we've already seen what he means when he says "walk," so we won't elaborate on that. But Paul goes on to give us more detail as to what it means to walk worthily, to live in holiness.

> With all lowliness and gentleness, with longsuffering, bearing one another in love, endeavoring to keep the unity of the Spirit in the bond of peace.
>
> -Ephesians 4:2-3

Sounds a lot like the fruit of the Spirit, the fruit of holiness. He elaborates on the theme of unity, pointing out that the apostles, prophets, evangelists, shepherds, and teachers were all given to build us up "till we all come to the unity of the faith" (v. 13). Then he gives us some more details about what walking should look like:

> This I say, therefore, and testify in the Lord, that you should no longer walk as the rest of the Gentiles walk, in the futility of their mind, having their understanding darkened, being alienated from the life of God, because of the ignorance that is in them, because of the blindness of their heart; who, being past feeling, have given themselves over to lewdness, to work all uncleanness with greediness.
>
> But you have not so learned Christ, if indeed you have heard Him and have been taught by Him, as the truth is in Jesus: that you put off, concerning your former conduct,

the old man which grows corrupt according to the deceitful lusts, and be renewed in the spirit of your mind, and that you put on the new man which was created according to God, in true righteousness and holiness.

-Ephesians 4:17-24

Specifically,

Therefore, putting away lying, "Let each one of you speak truth with his neighbor, for we are members of one another. "Be angry, and do not sin": do not let the sun go down on your wrath, nor give place to the devil. Let him who stole steal no longer, but rather let him labor, working with his hands what is good, that he may have something to give him who has need. Let no corrupt word proceed out of your mouth, but what is good for necessary edification, that it may impart grace to the hearers. And do not grieve the Holy Spirit of God, by whom you were sealed for the day of redemption. Let all bitterness, wrath, anger, clamor, and evil speaking be put away from you, with all malice. And be kind to one another, tenderhearted, forgiving one another, even as God in Christ forgave you.

Therefore be imitators of God as dear children. And walk in love, as Christ also has loved us and given Himself for us, an offering and a sacrifice to God for a sweet-smelling aroma.

-Ephesians 4:25-5:2

And now, another big to-don't list:

But fornication and all uncleanness or covetousness, let it not even be named among you, as is fitting for saints; neither filthiness, nor foolish talking, nor coarse jesting, which are not fitting, but rather giving of thanks.

-Ephesians 5:3-4

The list starts off with some "big" no-no's: *fornication* we've seen before; *uncleanness*, which is impurity of motives, lustful or extravagant living; and *filthiness*, which has to do with obscenity and a base character. Mixed into this list is *covetousness*, which we tend sometimes to dismiss as not all that bad. But it was bad enough to make the Top-10 list at Sinai. Greed, or an unholy desire to have more, is completely inconsistent with the Christian life.

Then the list turns to some items that might be seen by some as nitpicky. *Foolish talking* and *coarse jesting*, or crude joking, are not the behaviors of a maturing Christian. In contrast to foolish talking, Paul and Peter both wrote of the importance of being "sober." We should be talking about those things that are true, and noble, and just, and pure, and lovely (Phl 4:8). And what about coarse jesting? What do we allow ourselves to joke about, that is actually displeasing to the Father? What TV shows or movies or internet videos do we consume and endorse by our laughter, that are actually vulgar and out-of-step with holy living?

Paul then puts the exclamation point on this passage by once again notifying us of the judgment on these sins:

> For this you know, that no fornicator, unclean person, nor covetous man, who is an idolater, has any inheritance in the kingdom of Christ and God.
>
> -Ephesians 5:5

As in the letter to the Galatians (and Corinthians and Romans), he is writing to the Church! I cannot over-emphasize this. This is not a call to sinners to repent. This is a call to the Church— those who believe they have been justified—to refrain from these behaviors. Because those who behave in this way WILL NOT HAVE "any inheritance in the kingdom of Christ and God."

9

PHILIPPIANS

If the Corinthian church was Paul's class clown, the church at Philippi was his prize student. The Philippians were Paul's favorites. They were living right, they were diligent, they were godly. Why is it important that we know that? Because even in the letter to the most righteous church on the block, Paul still addresses issues of holiness. He doesn't give a long drawn-out to-don't list with major sins, like in the other letters. They're not engaging in those major sins. Instead, he provides a window for us to see the extent of the sanctification process.

Let's Get Down to the Nitty Gritty

Ok Philippians, ok mature Christian readers, good work. You've conquered the big sins! You used to be bound up in lust and sexual sin, you used to be greedy, you used to be angry, you used to be drunk and unruly, you used to be bitter and hold onto unforgiveness. But not any longer. You don't lose your temper anymore, you don't look at those indecent images anymore, you don't desire unholy things anymore. Praise the Lord! Now, let's get down to the nitty gritty. You've merely allowed the Lord to sculpt the general shape with a chain saw. Now it's time for the sandpaper to perfect you into the smooth and beautiful creature He expects you to become. It's time to understand how deep sanctification actually runs.

> Let nothing be done through selfish ambition or conceit, but in lowliness of mind let each esteem others better than himself. Let each of you look out not only for his own interests, but also for the interests of others.
>
> -Philippians 2:3-4

We're beginning to see what the Lord meant when He said "love your neighbor as yourself" (12:31). Love is preferential treatment, preferring others to yourself. That's not easy. In fact, it's impossible. We're not built to prefer others to ourselves. We're not built to look out not only for our own interests, but for others' also. It takes divine power to be able to do that. But that's precisely what we have, divine power! And that's precisely what we're supposed to use!

"Let each esteem others better than himself." When you look at other people, and specifically other believers, do you see all their faults? And when you look at yourself, do you overlook all your own faults? Esteeming others better than ourselves doesn't mean we ignore facts such as *that person lives in blatant unrepentant sin, whereas I do not*, but it does mean we attempt to see the best in people, we make allowances and offer mercy, we don't deceive ourselves into thinking we are less depraved or have less of a potential to mess up. Assume the best of your brother, until he proves you wrong. Assume the worst of yourself, until you prove yourself wrong.

Paul continues:

> Do all things without complaining and disputing, that you may become blameless and harmless, children of God without fault ...
>
> -Philippians 2:14-15a

Does that actually mean to do *all* things without complaining? I can't complain about my job? I can't complain about my wife? I can't complain about my kids? I can't complain about my church? I can't complain about the guy who just cut me off in traffic? Well, that's what it says. Ok, so if this is an imperative, a command of Scripture to us, then what does it mean if we do complain? It means we're in sin. And we cannot go on in that sin, we have to repent of it.

The Sin of Fear and Anxiety

Brace yourself for a tough truth. Especially if you suffer from fear and anxiety. Jesus commanded that we "fear not" (Matt 10:28-31; Luke 12:7,32). So if we fear, we sin. Likewise Paul writes in this letter:

> Be anxious for nothing ...
>
> -Philippians 4:6a

That is a command of Scripture. To ignore it is to sin. See, it's easy for us to look at certain "situations" such as fear and anxiety as merely "unfortunate," and we feel sorry for people who live in a state of fear or anxiety. We often view them as victims. And most often they are victims, in one way or another. And if you're struggling with fear and anxiety, I am sorry. I'm sorry you're not walking in freedom, I'm sorry for the places you've been hurt, I'm sorry you are not experiencing your full inheritance right now. But Christianity does not allow us to remain in victimhood; Christ delivers us from victimhood. We are told to be anxious for nothing. Then we're told how to be anxious for nothing:

> ... but in everything by prayer and supplication, with thanksgiving, let your requests be made known to God; and the peace of God, which surpasses all understanding, will guard your hearts and minds through Christ Jesus.
> -Philippians 4:6b-7

Make your requests known to God. "God, I'm struggling with anxiety. I need you to take that away from me!" But do it *with thanksgiving*. Don't withhold your thanks for the blessings you can point to in your life just because you're focused on all of the problems.

* * * * *

Do not steal, do not murder, do not commit adultery—we know all the big ones. But, do not fear? Do not be anxious? Do not complain? Do not do anything through selfish ambition? These were the exhortations to the Philippians. The to-don't list is digging down deeper. See, to be holy is not just to refrain from sin, it is to be set apart. The pursuit of holiness never ends. As soon as you get victory in one area, the Lord will expose another, less obvious, less grievous area. I'm positive there are attitudes and actions in my own life that I'm not even aware of yet, that the Lord will eventually ask me to turn over to Him. Once I conquer what He's highlighted already, He'll reveal the next layer of the onion He wishes to peel. That's holiness. It's not fun and games. It's total surrender, and total obedience. It's total dependence on Him, and total desire for Him, at the cost of forsaking all of self.

10
COLOSSIANS

The letter to the Colossians is like the ones to the Romans and the Ephesians in that they all three begin with a primarily doctrinal focus, and all three end with a primarily practical focus. The latter, practical half of this letter has much to say about holiness. But, like Ephesians, the former, doctrinal half is also sprinkled with major statements regarding the importance of holiness.

Reconciled for Holiness

Bookending the high Christology presented in verses 13-20 of the first chapter are two such statements. First, Paul and Timothy:

> ... do not cease to pray for you, and to ask that you may be filled with the knowledge of His will in all wisdom and spiritual understanding; that you may walk worthy of the Lord, fully pleasing Him, being fruitful in every good work and increasing in the knowledge of God; strengthened with

all might, according to His glorious power, for all patience and longsuffering with joy; giving thanks to the Father who has qualified us to be partakers of the inheritance of the saints in the light.

-Colossians 1:9b-12

Their prayer was not that the Colossians accept the resurrection of Jesus as a propositional truth, and then go on living life as they had always done. Their prayer was that the truth of the Gospel would transform the Colossians such that they would "walk worthy of the Lord, fully pleasing Him, being fruitful." We've seen this word *walk* before, of course. Paul emphasizes again here that, post-justification, the name of the game is *walking*. We can't walk worthy of Him, we can't be fully pleasing to Him, if we are not living in holiness. Holiness is the expectation.

And once again, "being fruitful" appears as a component of this lifestyle. We have seen in Romans 6 that our fruit is holiness, and we have seen in Galatians 5 that this fruit of holiness manifests in nine different ways, which we call the fruit of the Spirit. Here in Colossians 1, two of these manifest-ations—"longsuffering and joy"—are recalled.

To this is added that the purpose of our reconciliation is:

… to present you holy, blameless, and above reproach in His sight

-Colossians 1:22b

We are not reconciled just because God wanted to do something nice for us. We are not reconciled just because God wanted to show Himself off. We are not reconciled just so we can go to heaven. We are reconciled so that we can be "holy, blameless, and above reproach in His sight." That means living a life of holiness. We can't be holy, blameless, and above reproach if we're not holy, blameless, and above reproach! Yes, the Bible really does mean what it says! And yes, it really is that simple! We are reconciled to be holy!

Now notice the caveat in verse 23. You will be made blameless:

> if indeed you continue in the faith, grounded and steadfast, and are not moved away from the hope of the gospel which you heard...
>
> -Colossians 1:23a

We keep seeing these conditional statements. IF! There is a condition for salvation, and that is the *if* of "continuing in the faith." A single moment of "decision" for Christ does not a disciple make. It is a lifetime of continuing to "walk" worthy of the Lord that leads, in the end, to eternal life (See Rom 6:22).

How

As we transition to the "practical," back half of the letter, we immediately come upon what may be the single most important verse we will look at in this book: Colossians 3:2. By this time, I hope you're fully convinced that holiness is not optional. We're about half way through laying out the full case for that truth. And in so doing, we saw that, legally, we are able to walk in holiness because "sin shall not have dominion" over us (Rom 6:14). But knowing the fact that holiness is attainable, and actually knowing *how* to go about attaining it, are two different things. Colossians 3:2 gives us the key to unlock the *how to* of pursuing holiness.

Set your mind on things above, not on things on the earth.

-Colossians 3:2

It is absolutely imperative that we do not try to accomplish holiness on our own. We can't do it by relying on our own strength. That means that just "trying harder" is never the solution. We have to set our minds on things above. And not just things, but rather the Lord Himself. The way to conquer sin is to get your focus off of the sin and onto God. See, He does the work of purifying us from sin, but He only does the work as we look to Him, spend time with Him, meditate on Him. If our minds are set on the things of this world, we will never be transformed to be like Him. It's the old adage of "you are what you eat." In this case, you become what you focus on. When you focus on the things of the world, you become worldly, you become weak and carnal and spiritually malnourished. But when you focus on the Lord, you become like Him, you become strengthened spiritually, you become holy.

I believe the vast majority of Christians who struggle with sin or even just a general lukewarm faith, do so for a very simple reason: they have not set their minds on the things above. They have not immersed themselves in God. They don't pray, they don't read the Bible. Bible study is a chore, it's not prioritized, it's not a daily discipline. Prayer has been relegated to meal time and bed time, 5 minutes here, 5 seconds there. That simply won't cut it. To become holy, He must be our focus. We must pray continually. Set your mind on things above.

I asked the question in the first chapter on Romans 8, "What is your mind set on?" If your mind is set on the things of the flesh, then you are walking according to the flesh, and the promise of "no condemnation" is not yours. But if your mind is set on the things of the Spirit, then you are walking according to the Spirit, and the promise of "no condemnation" is yours. Colossians 3:2 repackages this teaching into an imperative statement: set your mind on things above. Do it! This is a command of Scripture. When we set our minds on things above, the things of the Spirit, God then does the work of transforming us into His image.

Once again, it's interesting to take note of those things in Scripture for which God is responsible, and those things for which we are responsible. There are things that we can't do, that God alone can do. But there are other things that we can do, that we alone are responsible for. And we have that kind of contrast here. We cannot rid ourselves of sin, we cannot do the work of becoming holy. Only God can do that. But notice our responsibility: set your mind on things above. That's on us. It doesn't say "allow Him to set your mind on things above." We are told to set our own minds. In other words, you are responsible for setting your own mind on Him. That, by the way, is what is called *faith*. We must have faith in Him. We must believe in Him. We must set our minds on Him. We must fully immerse ourselves in Him. We must fully devote ourselves to Him. When we turn our full attention to Him, He does all the "dirty work" of sanctification. He begins to change us from the inside out. And this is a process, this is progressive. We don't get frustrated in the process. We don't despair that we're not perfect, we trust Him that He is making us perfect, and will make us perfect. We don't focus on ourselves and the imperfections that remain, we focus on Him and the perfection that already exists in Him.

Therefore

Another major to-don't list follows "setting your mind." First, we are told that we should set our minds on things above *because* we are dead, and our true life is found in Him, in the heavenlies, in the world of the Spirit:

> If then you were raised with Christ, seek those things which are above, where Christ is, sitting at the right hand of God. Set your mind on things above, not on things on the earth. For you died, and your life is hidden with Christ in God. When Christ who is our life appears, then you also will appear with Him in glory.
>
> -Colossians 3:1-4

Then we are given a famous Pauline "therefore." Since the Christian life entails a heavenly mindset and not a worldly mindset, we should stop doing sinful things:

> Therefore put to death your members which are on earth: fornication, uncleanness, passion, evil desire, and covetousness, which is idolatry. Because of these things the wrath of God is coming upon the sons of disobedience, in which you yourselves once walked when you lived in them.
>
> But now you yourselves are to put off all these: anger, wrath, malice, blasphemy, filthy language out of your mouth. Do not lie to one another, since you have put off the old man with his deeds, and have put on the new man who is renewed in knowledge according to the image of Him who created him,
>
> -Colossians 3:5-10

We've seen some of these forbidden acts before. But to the list we now add *passion*, which entails depraved or vile passions, and *filthy language out of your mouth*, which is foul or obscene speech.

In the final call to holiness in this letter, another to-do list provides contrast against the previous to-don't list:

> Therefore, as the elect of God, holy and beloved, put on tender mercies, kindness, humility, meekness, long-suffering; bearing with one another, if anyone has a complaint against another; even as Christ forgave you, so you also must do. But above all these things put on love, which is the bond of perfection. And let the peace of God rule in your hearts, to which also you were called in one body; and be thankful.
>
> -Colossians 3:12-15

As followers of Jesus, we are to be kind, humble, meek, and longsuffering. We are to forgive others *as* we have been forgiven. We are to put on the love of God, and allow His peace to rule our hearts. And in all this, we are to be thankful. These are the characteristics of a life of holiness.

11
THESSALONIANS

The first letter to the Thessalonians is unlike any we've seen yet. Far from being an exposition of doctrine, or even a set of practical instructions for daily living, it instead basically reads a bit like a ministerial newsletter. For the most part, the letter chronicles Paul's recent activities, and particularly how they coincide with his thoughts and feelings toward the church at Thessalonica.

It is recounted how the Thessalonians' testimony was encouraging to the Macedonians and Achaians (1:7). Then Paul notes how he was treated poorly at Philippi (2:2). He reminds the Thessalonians that while he was with them, his conduct was above reproach, so that "they would walk worthy of God" (2:12). Paul wanted to return to Thessalonica, but was hindered from doing so (2:18). He was forced to stay in Athens, but was able to send Timothy to help establish and encourage them in their faith (3:1-2). Now, at the time of the writing of the letter, Timothy had returned to Paul with a good report from the

Thessalonians (3:6). As they close this "newsletter" portion of their communication, they offer a prayer for the church, which once again reveals how holiness is always in the foreground of Paul's thinking:

> And may the Lord make you increase and abound in love to one another and to all, just as we do to you, so that he may establish your hearts blameless in holiness ...
>
> -1 Thessalonians 3:12-13

So, the first three chapters (of five total) comprise Paul's personal thoughts about his own journey, and how it intersects with the Thessalonians. Changing gears in the final major section, 4:13-5:11, Paul clarifies his teaching on certain aspects of the end times.

Why have I gone through all this summary? Simply to make the point that even in this letter, even in a piece of writing that is neither theologically nor practically didactic in its focus, Paul nevertheless takes time to make a major statement on the importance of holiness. In between the "newsletter" and the "lesson on end times," he writes this:

> Finally then, brethren, we urge and exhort in the Lord Jesus that you should abound more and more, just as you received from us how you ought to walk and to please God; for you know what commandments we gave you through the Lord Jesus.
>
> -1 Thessalonians 4:1-2

Once again, Paul returns to his critically important theme of *walking*. And he says we "ought ... to please God." How so?

For this is the will of God, your sanctification: that you should abstain from sexual immorality; that each of you should know how to possess his own vessel in sanctification and honor, not in passion of lust, like the Gentiles who do not know God; that no one should take advantage of and defraud his brother in this matter, because the Lord is the avenger of all such, as we also forewarned you and testified. For God did not call us to uncleanness, but in holiness. Therefore, he who rejects this does not reject man, but God, who has also given us His Holy Spirit.

-1 Thessalonians 4:3-8

2 Thessalonians

The main idea of Paul's second letter to the Thessalonians seems to be to give even more clarity "concerning the coming of our Lord Jesus Christ and our gathering together to Him" (2:1). But even though the primary purpose for this letter is a teaching on end times, nevertheless the theme of holiness once again makes its way into the discourse in a couple of brief passages.

First, Paul writes that the Lord Jesus will take vengeance "in flaming fire" "on those who do not obey the gospel of our Lord" (1:8). Notice he doesn't say "on those who do not believe" but rather "on those who do not obey." Those who merely believe that the gospel is true, without actually obeying the gospel, do not seem to be found on the right side.

Second, Paul makes one of the most startling statements we've seen thus far near the end of chapter 2:

... God from the beginning chose you for salvation through sanctification ...

-2 Thessalonians 2:13

Salvation *through* sanctification?!? Can he really mean that? Is he really saying that salvation is more than just justification? That it's more than a singular event? Yep. We have been saved, we are being saved, and we will be saved. Those who are justified must move on through sanctification before arriving at glorification. Holiness is not optional. It will be developed in everyone who is truly saved and devoted to the Lord.

12
PAUL'S PERSONAL LETTERS

In Paul's personal correspondence (to individuals), holiness is not as much of a major theme as it is in his letters to the churches. Timothy and Titus, of course, were presumably living holy lives, and probably did not need to be reminded of the importance of holiness. And the letter to Philemon simply had a much different purpose, and did not warrant such a discussion. Nevertheless, even in Philemon we can infer some principles of Christian living that we might consider to be part of holiness, namely: mercy, love, and obedience. And in the letters to Timothy and Titus as well, we still see several references to holiness.

1 Timothy

At several points in the first letter, Paul exhorts Timothy to hold himself to a high standard of holiness. He tells him to have "faith and a good conscience" (1:19), to "be an example to the believers in word, in conduct, in love, in spirit, in faith, in purity" (4:12), to keep himself pure and not "share in other people's sins" (5:22), and to flee from greed and instead "pursue righteousness, godliness, faith, love, patience, gentleness" (6:11).

Timothy is also given instructions on how to spur the church on to holiness. He tells him several times to teach sound doctrine, and to ensure that others do the same. He commands that any elders who are sinning should be met with "rebuke in the presence of all" (5:20). And he further counsels, "withdraw yourself" from anyone who sees the ministry as a means of financial gain (6:5).

2 Timothy

Paul's admonitions to Timothy in the second letter are more robust, and consolidated into two main passages. First he writes:

> Be diligent to present yourself approved to God, a worker who does not need to be ashamed, rightly dividing the word of truth. But shun profane and idle babblings, for they will increase to more ungodliness. And their message will spread like cancer.
> ... Flee also youthful lusts; but pursue righteousness, faith, love, peace with those who call on the Lord out of a pure heart.
> -2 Timothy 2:15-17a, 22

Then we receive this warning about how holiness will wane in the last days:

> For men will be lovers of themselves, lovers of money, boasters, proud, blasphemers, disobedient to parents, un-thankful, unholy, unloving, unforgiving, slanderers, without self-control, brutal, despisers of good, traitors, headstrong,

haughty, lovers of pleasure rather than lovers of God, having a form of godliness but denying its power. And from such people turn away!

-2 Timothy 3:2-5

These people, Paul writes, are "disapproved concerning the faith" (3:8). But wait a minute. I thought all it took to go to heaven was faith. Hmm. It sure sounds like Paul is saying we need to be approved by God concerning our faith. Once again, faith is not about just believing a set of propositions, but rather proving our belief in Jesus through obedience to His commands. And those commands would include shunning the things on this list: loving yourself, loving money, boasting, pride, blaspheming, and on and on. Not only are we to refrain from these things, we are to turn away from even associating with people who claim citizenship in the kingdom of God, and yet practice these things!

Titus

At the end of Titus 1 we find a particularly useful passage for our study. Paul is warning Titus about the Judaizers who continue to want to add to the Gospel certain elements of the Jewish law such as circumcision. And the way he phrases his rejection of this practice helps us understand what it is that God is really looking for from us. Yes, He wants us to stop sinning; but more than that He wants us to be "pure" in our hearts.

To the pure all things are pure, but to those who are defiled and unbelieving nothing is pure; but even their mind and conscience are defiled. They profess to know God, but in works they deny Him, being abominable, disobedient, and disqualified for every good work.

-Titus 1:15-16

First let us see that it is possible to "profess to know God" and yet be "disqualified" because of "works" that "deny Him." This is just one more instance of Scripture confirming the truth of the consistent message of this book: it's not just a simple profession or belief in God that counts, but rather the faithful pursuit of obedience and holiness that proves our profession of faith.

But let's not miss the beginning of this thought. It is by "purity" that we have this assurance. In the end, it's really not our "works" that count. We will do good works, and we will refrain from doing bad works. And very likely from time to time we will miss the mark and do bad works. If we sin, that sin will not keep us from the Lord, it will not keep us from salvation. It's not the sins themselves that will cause us a problem (that is, an eternal problem). What will cause us an eternal problem is if we have an impure heart. It is those deep dark motives that most of us don't even realize are there. It is the heart that is not fully surrendered, that harbors iniquity, that insists on doing things "my way." We can even profess to know God, but if we are not truly surrendered in the deepest depths of our heart, we deceive ourselves. Being pure means I really do desire to please God in absolutely every dimension of my life. It doesn't mean I won't ever mess up. It means when I recognize something is amiss in my life, my attitude, my posture, I really am willing to turn that over to the Lord, and let Him be Lord! Those who are not pure in heart in this way are defiled, and "nothing is pure" for them. Even the good works they do will be burnt up.

The remainder of the letter is full of practical teaching on holiness, like the latter portions of most of Paul's letters to the churches. Titus is told to remind his sheep to behave well, "to be peaceable, gentle, showing all humility to all men" (3:2). We used to be "foolish, disobedient, deceived, serving various lusts and pleasures, living in malice and envy" (3:3). But because we have been redeemed, we should do these things no longer.

And here in the letter to Titus we find one of the most concise and thorough encapsulations of the necessity of holiness:

> For the grace of God that brings salvation has appeared to all men, teaching us that, denying ungodliness and worldly lusts, we should live soberly, righteously, and godly in the present age, looking for the blessed hope and glorious appearing of our great God and Savior Jesus Christ, who gave Himself for us, that He might redeem us from every lawless deed and purify for Himself His own special people, zealous for good works.
>
> -Titus 2:11-14

The "grace of God that brings salvation" teaches us that we should turn from the practices of the world and turn in full obedience to the Lord. I can't make it any more plain than this. We have been redeemed to be purified so that we may be zealous to do good works.

13
HEBREWS

Hebrews includes some of the clearest teachings on holiness in all of the epistles. It is primarily a manifesto designed to construct for the reader a high Christology and an explanation of the better, New Covenant. First, Jesus is greater than the angels. Second, He is greater than Moses. Third, He is greater than the priesthood. The covenant He came to ratify is greater than the former covenant, too. Therefore—beginning in Chapter 12 (the same message in the same location that it occurs in Romans)—we should live in holiness. And at each stop along this journey into the theology of the Son, we find an impassioned plea for the reader, in response to Christ's person and work, to give all diligence to living a holy life.

Opening Comparisons

Writing to a primarily Jewish audience, the author of Hebrews begins by making a case for the complete superiority of Jesus. He is the very Son of God, fully divine. And we are given proof of His superiority by way of a couple of comparisons to certain familiar characters who had a lot of respect in that community. First, we are told that Jesus is greater than *the angels*. And we know this because the angels in fact worship Him (1:6). At the beginning of Hebrews 2 a conclusion is drawn from the fact that Jesus is greater than the angels:

> Therefore we must give the more earnest heed to the things we have heard, lest we drift away. For if the word spoken through angels proved steadfast, and every transgression and disobedience received a just reward, how shall we escape if we neglect so great a salvation, which at the first began to be spoken by the Lord
> -Hebrews 2:1-3a

In other words, if disobedience to the word of the angels has been met with judgment in times past, how much more so will disobedience to the word of the Lord be met with judgment (since we have just shown that Christ is superior to the angels)?

The second comparison used to establish the superiority and sufficiency of the Son is the comparison of Jesus to Moses. We are asked to consider Jesus,

> Who was faithful to Him who appointed Him, as Moses also was faithful in all His house. For this One has been counted worthy of more glory than Moses, inasmuch as He who built the house has more honor than the house.
> -Hebrews 3:2-3

Given that Jesus is greater than Moses, we are given a Mosaic experience to serve as an example of what our postures should be in the New Covenant. Quoting the Psalmist, the writer of

Hebrews warns the reader, "Today, if you will hear His voice, do not harden your hearts as in the rebellion" (3:7-8). In the "trial of the wilderness," the Israelites tested and tried God. And He was angry with them, and swore in His wrath, "They shall not enter My rest" (3:8-11). Again, the conclusion is sobering:

> Beware, brethren, lest there be in any of you an evil heart of unbelief in departing from the living God; but exhort one another daily, while it is still called "Today," lest any of you be hardened through the deceitfulness of sin. For we have become partakers of Christ if we hold the beginning of our confidence steadfast to the end, while it is said:
>
> "Today, if you will hear His voice,
> Do not harden your hearts as in the rebellion."
>
> For who, having heard, rebelled? Indeed, was it not all who came out of Egypt, led by Moses? Now with whom was He angry forty years? Was it not with those who sinned, whose corpses fell in the wilderness? And to whom did He swear that they would not enter His rest, but to those who did not obey? So we see that they could not enter in because of unbelief.
>
> -Hebrews 3:12-19

Ok, let's work through this passage. First of all, we are warned not to enter into "unbelief" by departing from the faith (v. 12). Our hearts can be hardened by sin (v. 13). And we only have assurance of salvation "IF" we continue steadfastly in the faith to the end (v. 14). Then it's made explicit: those who did not enter His rest were those who did not *obey* (v. 18). Obedience is the key! And don't miss this: "so we see that they could not enter in because of unbelief." In other words, disobedience and unbelief are equated. We are given insight into the nature of this difficult concept called *believing*. It is not a mere "intellectual assent to a set of scriptural propositions," it is *obedience*. They did not enter His rest because of disobedience, that is, because of unbelief.

Having set forth the Mosaic example, the author drives home the new-covenant application in Chapter 4:

> Therefore, since a promise remains of entering His rest, let
> us fear lest any of you seem to have come short of it.
> -Hebrews 4:1

The Israelites had a promise of rest called the promised land. We also have a promise of rest called eternal life. As they missed out on their promised rest because of disobedience/unbelief, "let us fear" so that we don't make the same mistake. Let us fear, meaning, let's not approach this thing lightly, let's be sober and diligent to obey always.

> There remains therefore a rest for the people of God. ...
> Let us therefore be diligent to enter that rest, lest anyone
> fall according to the same example of disobedience.
> -Hebrews 4:9, 11

It is quite clear from this passage that disobedience will keep us from entering the eternal rest, but diligence in obedience will be rewarded with eternal rest.

Judgment for the Rejection of the Sacrifice

Over the next five chapters, the author goes on to lay out many specifics about the nature of the New Covenant: how

Jesus is the High Priest and Mediator of that covenant, how the priests and sacrifices of the Mosaic model are no longer necessary, how Jesus' sacrifice—once and for all—is all that is necessary to inherit the promises of the New Covenant. It is in this context that the following warning is issued:

> For if we sin willfully after we have received the knowledge of the truth, there no longer remains a sacrifice for sins, but a certain fearful expectation of judgment, and fiery indignation which will devour the adversaries. Anyone who has rejected Moses' law dies without mercy on the testimony of two or three witnesses. Of how much worse punishment, do you suppose, will he be thought worthy who has trampled the Son of God underfoot, counted the blood of the covenant by which he was sanctified a common thing, and insulted the Spirit of grace? For we know Him who said, "Vengeance is Mine, I will repay," says the Lord. And again, "The LORD will judge His people." It is a fearful thing to fall into the hands of the living God.
>
> -Hebrews 10:26-31

I wish I could emphasize this passage with 100 exclamation marks. I said it at the beginning of this book. Do you really think God has changed?! Not one iota. If He had a zero-tolerance policy for sin in the Old Covenant, do you really believe He will tolerate it in the New Covenant?! Don't bet your life on it! "The LORD will judge His people. It is a fearful thing to fall into the hands of the living God."

Final Thoughts

Like many other letters we have seen, the end of Hebrews contains some practical application of the doctrine laid out in the first 11 chapters. We are given commands such as, "Let brotherly love continue" (13:1), "be content" (13:5), and "obey those who rule over you" (13:17).

In light of every truth penned in this masterpiece, we are instructed to lay aside "the sin which so easily ensnares us" (12:1). We are given insight into how zealous we should be to overcome sin: "You have not yet resisted to bloodshed, striving against sin" (12:4). And finally, we are given the most straightforward statement yet regarding the necessity of holiness:

> Pursue peace with all people, and holiness, without which no one will see the Lord
>
> -Hebrews 12:14

Without holiness, no one will see the Lord. Let me say it one more time. Without holiness, no one will see the Lord. Ladies and gentlemen, I may have eight chapters remaining, nevertheless I am fully prepared at this point to rest my case: *Holiness is Not Optional.*

14

JAMES

James is often contrasted with Paul, and that contrast is often taken too far, with Paul being cast as the *faith proponent* while James is relegated to the *works proponent*. But of course we have already seen that Paul is very much in favor of works. And we have seen what sort of works he is in favor of—not works of the Law, but works born of faith. And that is exactly what kind of works James is interested in. It is not an overstatement to say that the main idea of James' letter is that we should operate in that kind of faith that is evidenced by works, and that any other kind of faith is not really faith at all, at least not a saving faith. I would guess that the sloppy grace proponents would be just as happy to take James out of the canon altogether rather than read him and take him at face value. But taking him at face value is precisely what I intend to do.

Don't be Deceived

It doesn't take long for James to settle into the message of abstaining from sin and practicing good works.

> So then, my beloved brethren, let every man be swift to hear, slow to speak, slow to wrath; for the wrath of man does not produce the righteousness of God.
>
> Therefore lay aside all filthiness and overflow of wickedness, and receive with meekness the implanted word, which is able to save your souls.
>
> But be doers of the word, and not hearers only, deceiving yourselves. For if anyone is a hearer of the word and not a doer, he is like a man observing his natural face in a mirror; for he observes himself, goes away, and immediately forgets what kind of man he was.
>
> -James 1:19-24

He says that anyone who fails to *do* what the Word requires is deceiving himself. That's where many of us are, aren't we? We know right from wrong, and we know what we're supposed to do and what we're supposed to refrain from doing, but we often do the opposite. The more we "do" that is out of alignment with His commands, the further and further we move into deception, where it becomes harder and harder to come back to righteousness.

Then we get a few examples:

> If anyone among you thinks he is religious, and does not bridle his tongue but deceives his own heart, this one's religion is useless. Pure and undefiled religion before God and the Father is this: to visit orphans and widows in their trouble, and to keep oneself unspotted from the world.
>
> -James 1:26-27

One of the things entailed in being a "doer" is to keep control of your tongue. You are in deception if you think your religion is meritorious, and yet you speak in a way that is un-Christlike. Then we get a statement that sums up the two prongs of mature Christian living: service and holiness. Visiting widows and orphans is an example of service (to the Lord and to others). And of course, keeping oneself unspotted from the world is another way of saying keeping oneself sin-free, or, holy.

Faith Plus Works

In Chapter 2 we get the core of James' faith-works teaching. He asks:

> What does it profit, my brethren, if someone says he has faith but does not have works? Can faith save him? If a brother or sister is naked and destitute of daily food, and one of you says to them, "Depart in peace, be warmed and filled," but you do not give them the things which are needed for the body, what does it profit? Thus also faith by itself, if it does not have works, is dead.
>
> But someone will say, "You have faith, and I have works." Show me your faith without your works, and I will show you my faith by my works. You believe that there is one God. You do well. Even the demons believe—and tremble! But do you want to know, O foolish man, that faith without works is dead?
>
> -James 2:14-20

Here we see another indication of what kind of faith, what kind of believing is the kind that yields eternal results. Even the demons believe! That kind of belief—belief that God exists, that He is good and holy and all-powerful, or even that He will win in the end—is not the kind of belief that saves. It is faith that produces good works that justifies.

James gives two examples of individuals who were justified by works: Abraham, who offered Isaac on the altar, and Rahab, who helped the messengers escape. And he punctuates the entire passage with this startling assertion:

> You see then that a man is justified by works, and not by faith only.
>
> -James 2:24

To hear the sloppy grace proponents talk, you wouldn't know this verse even existed. In fact, there's very little room in modern evangelicalism in general for serious contemplation of this verse. "By grace through faith" has been propped up as the sum total of the salvation plan. And although, in a way, it is, we must understand what exactly is meant by those words *grace* and *faith*. And James helps us to get that clarity. Grace empowers us to live in holiness, and it is through a faith evidenced by works that we lay hold of this grace.

Motives Run Deep

James gets a little more personal in Chapter 4. It's not enough for us to simply know that we must do good works. Holiness, at its core is not about deeds—neither the good ones we do nor the bad ones we don't do. Deep down it really is a matter of the heart, it is a matter of motives.

> Where do wars and fights come from among you? Do they not come from your desires for pleasure that war in your members? You lust and do not have. You murder and

covet and cannot obtain. You fight and war. Yet you do not have because you do not ask. You ask and do not receive, because you ask amiss, that you may spend it on your pleasures. Adulterers and adulteresses! Do you not know that friendship with the world is enmity with God? Whoever therefore wants to be a friend of the world makes himself an enemy of God.

-James 4:1-4

How many times have we who claim to "follow" the Lord operated according to our own pleasures, often even unaware of the problem. How friendly with the world are we really? And have we made ourselves enemies of God through our friendship with the world?

Therefore submit to God. Resist the devil and he will flee from you. Draw near to God and He will draw near to you. Cleanse your hands, you sinners; and purify your hearts, you double-minded. Lament and mourn and weep! Let your laughter be turned to mourning and your joy to gloom. Humble yourselves in the sight of the Lord, and He will lift you up.

-James 4:7-10

How often have we quoted James 4:8? Draw near to God, and He will draw near to you. Have you tried drawing near only to find that you did not feel Him draw near to you? Is it possible that He did not draw near because you failed to cleanse your hands and purify your heart? Lament and mourn and weep! Now that's a prescription that today's pastors are not willing to share from their pulpits. We want happiness, we want to feel good, we want success, we want to "move forward in the things of God." We wouldn't dream of lamenting and mourning and weeping over the sin that remains in our lives, the ugly motives that still block our path to total freedom and unbridled power of the Spirit. This is not figurative, and it's not hyperbole! Lament and mourn and weep! Start shedding tears over unconquered sin. Humble yourself in the sight of the Lord.

15
THE PETRINE EPISTLES

If Paul's letters may be generally described as a main course of doctrine with a side of practical application, perhaps Peter's letters may be described as a main course of practical teachings for daily living with a side of doctrine. Romans, for example, opens with 11 chapters of doctrine that give way to the "therefore" that marks the beginning of the practical application that spans only 3 chapters. By contrast, the "therefore" of 1 Peter occurs after only 12 verses (1:13), and is followed by 4½ chapters worth of a candid depiction of proper Christian living. As you might imagine, where one of the major apostolic voices of the early church teaches us what daily life should look like, holiness emerges as a major component of the lessons.

1 Peter

Peter opens his first letter by praising God for our "living hope" that is only possible "through the resurrection of Jesus Christ from the dead" (1:3). This great salvation, he explains, comes to completion after "the genuineness of your faith" is "tested" by "various trials" (1:6-7). And here is the conclusion he arrives at based on these spiritual facts:

> Therefore gird up the loins of your mind, be sober, and rest your hope fully upon the grace that is to be brought to you at the revelation of Jesus Christ; as obedient children, not conforming yourselves to the former lusts, as in your ignorance; but as He who called you is holy, you also be holy in all your conduct, because it is written, "Be holy, for I am holy."
>
> -1 Peter 1:13-16

The logical outworking of our salvation is holiness. In obedience, we are not to continue in our "former lusts," but rather to "be holy." It may seem impossible, or even insane, that we should make an effort to be holy "as" He is holy. Surely we can never be holy as He is holy. But then again, why would Scripture tell us to be exactly that? Because that is exactly what the Gospel empowers us to do! We *can* be holy as He is holy. And we should live our lives in constant pursuit of that goal.

Peter continues, laying out a to-don't list not unlike those of Paul, instructing us to lay aside "all malice, all deceit, hypocrisy, envy, and all evil speaking" (2:1). We are told to "abstain from fleshly lusts" so that our reputation in the world around us will remain untarnished. In fact, they should "think it strange" that we have undergone such a transformation of sanctification, because in our past life, we acted just as they did, walking in "lewdness, lusts, drunkenness, revelries, drinking parties, and abominable idolatries" (4:3-4).

The letter closes with a call to sobriety as the means of faithfully carrying out the difficult task of living the Christian life:

Be sober, be vigilant; because your adversary the devil walks about like a roaring lion, seeking whom he may devour. Resist him, steadfast in the faith

-1 Peter 5:8-9a

That sure sounds like more than a simple "decision" for Christ. That sounds like Christian living requires perseverance. In fact, it sounds like the kind of "faith" that is not steadfast, is not contended for, is not pursued with vigilance, is not a saving kind of faith at all, but rather some illusion of a weak and deceived individual who can easily be devoured by the enemy. Have mercy, Lord, that it may not be us!

2 Peter

Peter's main concerns in his second letter seem to be to urge his readers to contend against heretical doctrines (Chapter 2) and to remind them that there will indeed be a final judgment (Chapter 3). These two ideas are linked together, since many who are promulgating false doctrine are doing so by implying that the Lord will not return because "all things continue as they were from the beginning of creation" (3:4).

What is interesting, for our purposes, is that even though exhortation to holiness is not one of the primary purposes of the letter, it nevertheless dominates the entire first chapter. We conclude from this that holiness is such an essential component of the message of Christianity, that for Peter, it is critical that we be reminded of it as frequently as possible. Here is how Peter conveys the message:

> His divine power has given us everything required for life and godliness
>
> -2 Peter 1:3a (CSB)

God empowers, and God does the work in us. That's grace. And through His power, He makes a way of

> escaping the corruption that is in the world because of evil desire.
>
> -2 Peter 1:4b (CSB)

In other words, He empowers us to overcome sin. In so doing, we walk according to the Spirit, and we are free from condemnation.

> For this very reason, make every effort to supplement your faith with goodness, goodness with knowledge, knowledge with self-control, self-control with endurance, endurance with godliness, godliness with brotherly affection, and brotherly affection with love. For if you possess these qualities in increasing measure, they will keep you from being useless or unfruitful in the knowledge of our Lord Jesus Christ. The person who lacks these things is blind and shortsighted and has forgotten the cleansing from his past sins. Therefore, brothers and sisters, make every effort to confirm your calling and election, because if you do these things you will never stumble. For in this way, entry into the eternal kingdom of our Lord and Savior Jesus Christ will be richly provided for you.
>
> -2 Peter 1:5-11 (CSB)

Supplement your faith?! That sounds like heresy! I thought we were saved by faith alone. Make every effort?! I thought we were just supposed to rely on God to do everything. Confirm your calling and election?! Are we called and elected or not? I thought it was a done deal and all I had to do was just "accept" it! Ladies and gentlemen, once again there is more to this idea of "faith" than we see at first glance. Yes, it is faith alone that saves, by grace, but it is a specific kind of faith. It is that kind of faith that leads to goodness and knowledge and self-control and endurance and godliness and brotherly affection and love. "If you do these things you will never stumble." For it is "IN THIS WAY" that we gain "entry into the eternal kingdom." You do not gain entry into the eternal kingdom merely by responding to an altar call. You gain entry into the eternal kingdom *in this way*: by making every effort to pursue the things of the Lord from this day forward for the rest of your life.

16

THE JOHANNINE EPISTLES

Three letters from the Apostle John are included in the New Testament canon. In the first and most substantial, John wants to get across two major thoughts: 1) love one another, and 2) be on guard against the spirit of antichrist that claims that Jesus did not come in the flesh. The second letter is basically a condensed version of the first, echoing these same two points, in fewer words. The third letter, as it is a personal correspondence with Gaius and not a general letter to the church, is different in its focus—essentially a note of encouragement to a friend. Letters two and three are so short that they don't include much in relation to holiness, although the theme is surely not absent. In 2 John we are told to "love one another," and that what it means to love one another is to "walk according to His commandments" (vv. 5-6). Clearly this is simply another way to say what Paul has already drilled into us: "walk according to the Spirit." And in 3 John we are instructed not to "imitate what is evil, but what is good." This command is clarified by a rather cut-and-dried statement: "He who does good is of God, but he who does evil has not seen God" (v. 11). This simple idea that we can easily discern who is of God and who isn't, based on peoples' actions, is developed more extensively in 1 John, which we will turn to now.

Conditionals

John's first letter is filled with if-then statements, which tend to portray the world in black and white.

> If we say that we have fellowship with Him, and walk in darkness, we lie and do not practice the truth. But if we walk in the light as He is in the light, we have fellowship with one another, and the blood of Jesus Christ His Son cleanses us from all sin.
>
> -1 John 1:6-7

Notice again the word *walk*. John, too, equates walking with righteousness. You can say that you're a Christian, but if you walk in darkness, if your walk is according to the flesh and not according to the Spirit, then you are a liar. The way we know we are cleansed from all sin is if we walk in the light, which is another way to say we walk according to the Spirit.

He continues:

> My little children, I am writing you these things so that you may not sin. But if anyone does sin, we have an advocate with the Father—Jesus Christ the righteous one.
>
> -1 John 2:1 (CSB)

First of all, it is comforting to know that if we do sin, we have someone to turn to for help. Jesus goes before the Father on our behalf, and "if we confess our sins, he is faithful and just to forgive us our sins, and cleanse us from all unrighteousness" (1:9). However, we should also note the implications of the phrase "if anyone does sin." Why does he not instead say "when anyone sins"? For the very simple reason that for the sanctified believer, it is not a foregone conclusion that we will sin! As I said earlier, I am convinced that at the moment of conversion, the Holy Spirit comes to take up residence in the believer, empowering us so that, hypothetically, *it is possible to never sin again.* Now, most of us don't actually walk that out. But that is what the Holy Spirit empowers us to do, to live sin-free. And that's what John is saying here. "If anyone does sin" implies that we don't have to. And certainly it indicates that sin should not be the norm of our lives.

The black-and-white conditional statements continue on in Chapter 2:

> Now by this we know that we know Him, if we keep His commandments. He who says "I know Him," and does not keep His commandments, is a liar, and the truth is not in him. But whoever keeps His word, truly the love of God is perfected in him. By this we know that we are in Him. He who says he abides in Him ought himself also to walk just as He walked.
>
> -1 John 2:3-6

We know Him if we keep His commandments, if we live according to His dictates. If we don't keep His commandments, we don't know Him. Black and white. And how do we know that we are in Him? We ought to walk just as He walked. Wow, that sounds like a tall order. Can we really walk just as Jesus walked? The short answer is *yes.* We will never be divine, we can never be who Jesus was and is. But we are supposed to imitate Him and be like Him. And by the power of the Holy Spirit, we can live a life that closely resembles the life Jesus lived.

In Chapter 3, John explains more of the stark contrast between those who sin and those who live sin-free.

> Whoever commits sin also commits lawlessness, and sin is lawlessness. And you know that He was manifested to take away our sins, and in Him there is no sin. Whoever abides in Him does not sin. Whoever sins has neither seen Him nor known Him.
>
> Little children, let no one deceive you. He who practices righteousness is righteous, just as He is righteous. He who sins is of the devil, for the devil has sinned from the beginning. For this purpose the Son of God was manifested, that He might destroy the works of the devil. Whoever has been born of God does not sin, for His seed remains in him; and he cannot sin, because he has been born of God.
>
> -1 John 3:4-9

"For this purpose." John makes another black-and-white statement, that people who practice righteousness are righteous, and people who sin are of the devil. (Notice this is a statement regarding conduct, not beliefs.) And in the context of this he says that the *purpose* of Jesus' descent to earth was to destroy the works of the devil. In other words, Jesus came not only to set us free from the guilt of sin, but also to set us free from the power of sin. Not only so we could have right beliefs, but so we could have righteous deeds. His finished work is a work of empowering us to not sin! This is how we know we are His, if we, by His Spirit, practice righteousness and eschew sin.

This epistle is quite repetitive, and several of the concepts we've seen already, as well as the ones to come, are reinforced multiple times throughout. One such repetition, which comes at the end of the letter, gives us a key to walking in the light:

> We know that whoever is born of God does not sin, but he who has been born of God keeps himself, and the wicked one does not touch him.
>
> -1 John 5:18

"Whoever is born of God does not sin!" Instead, he keeps himself. That word *keeps* means *to attend carefully* or *to guard*. We are to attend carefully to our souls, continually guarding ourselves from anything that would lead us away from the things of God. This is how one who is born of God lives, in steadfast faithfulness.

Love One Another

In addition to keeping His commandments, we learn in 1 John that walking in the light also entails loving one another.

> He who says he is in the light, and hates his brother, is in darkness until now. He who loves his brother abides in the light, and there is no cause for stumbling in him.
>
> -1 John 2:9-10

Do you really love people? Do you care about others? Pray for others? Help others? Reach out to see how they're doing? Do you invest in other people even though there may not be a return on your investment? Do you love other people for their own sake?

John drives this point home on several occasions throughout the letter. By the end, there should be no mistaking that true believers in Jesus should be marked by a supernatural love that they have for one another.

> We know that we have passed from death to life, because we love the brethren. He who does not love his brother abides in death. Whoever hates his brother is a murderer, and you know that no murderer has eternal life abiding in him.
>
> By this we know love, because He laid down His life for us. And we also ought to lay down our lives for the brethren. But whoever has this world's goods, and sees his brother in need, and shuts up his heart from him, how does the love of God abide in him?
>
> My little children, let us not love in word or in tongue, but in deed and in truth.
>
> -1 John 3:14-18

> Beloved, let us love one another, for love is of God; and everyone who loves is born of God and knows God. He who does not love does not know God, for God is love.
>
> -1 John 4:7-8

> If someone says, "I love God," and hates his brother, he is a liar; for he who does not love his brother whom he has seen, how can he love God whom he has not seen? And this commandment we have from Him: that he who loves God must love his brother also.
>
> -1 John 4:20-21

Do Not Love the World

One final point in the teachings of John remains to be considered. Besides the love that we should have for one another, John makes a point to tell us that there is a love that we should *not* have: love for the world.

> Do not love the world or the things in the world. If anyone loves the world, the love of the Father is not in him. For all that is in the world—the lust of the flesh, the lust of the eyes, and the pride of life—is not of the Father but is of the world.
>
> -1 John 2:15-16

If you love the world, or the things in the world, the love of the Father is not in you. Now, that doesn't mean that we cannot take joy in the simple pleasures of life. But it does mean that if we are children of God, we cannot begin to elevate worldly things above the things of God. How much do you love your phone? Social media? Sports? Entertainment? How much do you crave attention or fame or wealth or material goods? John is telling us that the things of the world speak directly to our carnal desires, which come in one of three forms: the lust of the flesh, the lust of the eyes, and the pride of life. Worldly things will feel good, or look good, or build up our pride. But they will not be pleasing to God.

We are told to not love the world. That's not easy, because the world is easy to love. There are so many things in it that can steal our attention, steal our desires, and steal our dedication to the Lord. That's why John says later that we should "keep" ourselves. We have to be on guard, we have to attend carefully to our souls. Living the Christian life is a continual posturing of the heart toward God, and a continual consecration of the will against the enticement of the world.

17
JUDE

Jude is one of the shortest books in the Bible, and since I'm addressing it by itself here, it will certainly be the shortest chapter in this book. Nevertheless, even in the short span of 461 (Greek) words, Jude's emphasis on holiness should not go unnoticed.

Even the greeting indicates the need to be holy. The letter is written "to those who are called, sanctified by God the Father, and preserved in Jesus Christ" (v. 1). *Sanctified* literally means "holy-fied," so, as the reader, holiness is pre-requisite to even have the confidence that the letter is addressed to you.

Jude goes on to exhort his readers to "contend earnestly for the faith" (v. 3) because certain men had begun to creep in and distort the gospel such that they were "turn[ing] the grace of our God into lewdness" (v. 4). In other words, Jude is warning us to contend against a "sloppy grace" teaching that says that our freedom in Christ means that we have freedom to live in impurity.

Jude gives three examples of characters-of-old whose sin did not go unpunished—the angels who rebelled and left their place in heaven, the Israelites who came out of Egypt and yet did not make it to the promised land, and the ungodly residents of Sodom and Gomorrah—and he says that these "are set forth as an example" to us, the church (v. 7)! In other words, it's not only unsaved sinners who need to fear judgment, but also we who claim the name of Christ and yet continue to walk in ungodliness.

He then outlines some characteristics of these people. They "defile the flesh, reject authority, and speak evil of dignitaries" (v. 8). They are "grumblers, complainers, walking according to their own lusts; and they mouth great swelling words, flattering people to gain advantage" (v. 16). And to drive the point home once again, these are not people of the world, but people within the church, as Jude notes that they are "spots in your love feasts, while they feast with you without fear, serving only themselves" (v. 12).

But Jude does end this little letter of warning with an encouraging thought. Even though the journey is not easy, and our life of faith requires persistence and sobriety, we can be confident, because God "is able to keep you from stumbling, and to present you faultless before the presence of His glory" (v. 24). Praise the Lord! As we continue to set our minds on Him, He will do the work of keeping us in the faith!

18

REVELATION

On the one hand, it may be obvious that the teachings of Revelation show the necessity of holiness. After all, we learn from the book that Jesus will return to judge all mankind, and that those who are found in Him will be rewarded with eternal life, and those who have rejected Him will be rewarded with eternal damnation. On the other hand, the apocalyptic narrative itself does not say much about *how* one comes to be counted among the saved. Those who are written in the Lamb's book of life, are they written there because they merely *believed that* Jesus died for them? Or are they written there because they *believed in* Jesus to empower them to conquer sin and live in a manner worthy of Him? Certainly we've seen this question answered in the epistles. But if we want to find what Revelation has to say about it, it's not the apocalyptic portion itself we need to turn to, but rather the beginning section of the book, in which John records Jesus' words to the seven churches.

To the Angel of the Church in Ephesus Write

Jesus opens His revelation to John by exhorting seven churches in Asia Minor. Most of them were doing some things well. But most of them were also doing some things very poorly. The things they did poorly, the response Jesus required of them, and the penalty they would have to pay for not responding correctly to Jesus' rebuke: these three things are what we are most concerned with here.

Jesus praised the church in Ephesus for their patience, their discernment, and their labors. Nevertheless He finds fault with them on this count:

> you have left your first love. Remember therefore from where you have fallen; repent and do the first works, or else I will come to you quickly and remove your lampstand from its place—unless you repent.
>
> -Revelation 2:4-5

We don't get a lot of detail about the nature of the problem the Ephesians are having, only simply that they have left their first love, and they need to return to doing their "first works." It seems, based on their list of good qualities, that they had perhaps begun to get caught up more in the work of the church than being caught up in relationship with the Lord Himself. That certainly is a trap that today's churches can easily fall into. How many are more concerned about the work of their church, the growth of their church, the success of their church, than they are with the real concerns of the Spirit?

The solution to the Ephesian problem is *repentance.* And the penalty for not repenting is steep: their lampstand will be removed. Now Jesus has already explained in Chapter 1 that the lampstand signifies the church itself. So if their lampstand is removed, literally the church-ness of the church is removed. They will cease to be a legitimate church, fully sanctioned and ordained of the Lord.

This brief passage shows us how sobering our task truly is. Not only must we renounce sin, but we must also maintain our first love. Simply doing the works of the Lord is not enough; these works must be done from a heart of love for Him.

To the Angel of the Church in Smyrna Write

Jesus had no criticisms of the church in Smyrna. They had good works, they faithfully endured tribulation, and they had a humility that made them rich in the things of God. Even though there is no "correction" to this church that would give us a lesson in the necessity of living right, there is nevertheless one sentence that reinforces our theme: "Be faithful until death, and I will give you the crown of life" (v. 10). By itself this statement may not mean much, but given the extensive evidence we have seen so far for the necessity of holiness, this little statement just adds one more layer of support. We are rewarded with the crown of life by being faithful unto death. We must persevere to the end. A "decision" for Christ means nothing if we do not see that decision through in a lifetime of faithfulness.

More Churches, More Grievances

Most of the remaining churches had similar issues to the first. Only the churches in Smyrna and Philadelphia were completely above reproach. The other churches all had different issues, but they each had their issues. They are all praised for what they do well, but they are rebuked for what they lack.

The church in Pergamos is corrected for holding:

> the doctrine of Balaam, who taught Balak to put a stumbling block before the children of Israel, to eat things sacrificed to idols, and to commit sexual immorality.
>
> -Revelation 2:14b

The church in Thyatira allowed:

> that woman Jezebel, who calls herself a prophetess, to teach and seduce My servants to commit sexual immorality and eat things sacrificed to idols.
>
> -Revelation 2:20b

The church in Sardis had a reputation for being alive, but they were actually dead. And they were cautioned:

> Be watchful, and strengthen the things which remain, that are ready to die, for I have not found your works perfect before God. Remember therefore how you have received and heard; hold fast and repent. Therefore if you will not watch, I will come upon you as a thief, and you will not know what hour I will come upon you. You have a few names even in Sardis who have not defiled their garments; and they shall walk with Me in white, for they are worthy.
>
> -Revelation 3:2-4

Because of their sin, the Lord will come upon them "as a thief," reminiscent of Peter's description of the day of the Lord (2Pe 3:10). Here, an event we normally think of as reserved for the "ungodly," is being attributed to the unfaithful church. And we see also that some in Sardis are living in holiness, and it is these who will "walk in white;" the clear implication is that those who do not keep themselves holy will not walk with Him in white. Finally, to the church of the Laodiceans, Jesus says this:

> I know your works, that you are neither cold nor hot. I could wish you were cold or hot. So then, because you are lukewarm, and neither cold nor hot, I will vomit you out of My mouth. Because you say, "I am rich, have become wealthy, and have need of nothing"—and do not know that you are wretched, miserable, poor, blind, and naked—I counsel you to buy from Me gold refined in the fire, that you may be rich; and white garments, that you may be clothed, that the shame of your nakedness may not be revealed; and anoint your eyes with eye salve, that you may see. As many as I love, I rebuke and chasten. Therefore be zealous and repent.
>
> -Revelation 3:15-19

I fear this passage describes the American church today to a T. We have become so rich that we have need of nothing. And if we're not careful, we can easily mistake having no need for anything as having no need for God. He simply becomes an add-on, a little piece of our lives that we pay lip-service to, but never seek with desperation. The fact is, we do have need of something, of Someone. It's not too late, America. Because He loves you, He rebukes and chastens you. "Therefore be zealous and repent."

A Consistent Theme to the Churches

One final thought about the words to the churches. They all end with a comment about overcoming. It is to the *overcomer* that the reward of eternal life is granted. It's not to the one who simply agrees that the Word of God is true, it's not to the one who asks for forgiveness and yet goes on sinning, it's not to the one who merely believes without acting. It's to the one who lives out a lifetime of faithfulness to the Lord.

> To him who overcomes I will give to eat from the tree of life, which is in the midst of the Paradise of God.
>
> -Revelation 2:7b

> He who overcomes shall not be hurt by the second death.
>
> -Revelation 2:11b

> To him who overcomes I will give some of the hidden manna to eat.
>
> -Revelation 2:17b

> And he who overcomes, and keeps My works until the end, to him I will give power over the nations—
>
> -Revelation 2:26

> He who overcomes shall be clothed in white garments, and I will not blot out his name from the Book of Life; but I will confess his name before My Father and before His angels.
>
> -Revelation 3:5

> He who overcomes, I will make him a pillar in the temple of My God, and he shall go out no more. I will write on him the name of My God and the name of the city of My God, the New Jerusalem, which comes down out of heaven from My God. And I will write on him My new name.
>
> -Revelation 3:12

To him who overcomes I will grant to sit with Me on My throne, as I also overcame and sat down with My Father on His throne.

-Revelation 3:21

The Final Judgment

We have seen that holiness is not optional. We have seen that sanctification, in addition to justification, is part of the process of salvation. But we have not said much about the consequences. What if I'm not holy? What if I am that person who once responded to an altar call long ago, but didn't really walk away from that point of decision truly changed? What if I am that person who has gone through the motions of church and religion, and yet never submitted my heart fully to the Lord? What if I don't walk according to the Spirit, but I do walk according to the flesh? What if I'm not one who has overcome?

Well, the book of Revelation answers those questions. And not in gentle or encouraging terms. There will be a judgment day. Satan and his legion will be judged and sentenced. And so will every person who does not follow Jesus as Lord. Yes, even those who have at one point or another claimed His name.

The devil, who deceived them, was cast into the lake of fire and brimstone where the beast and the false prophet are. And they will be tormented day and night forever and ever.

Then I saw a great white throne and Him who sat on it, from whose face the earth and the heaven fled away. And there was found no place for them. And I saw the dead, small and great, standing before God, and books were opened. And another book was opened, which is the Book of Life. And the dead were judged according to their works, by the things which were written in the books. The sea gave up the dead who were in it, and Death and Hades delivered up the dead who were in them. And they were judged, each one according to his works. Then Death and Hades were cast into the lake of fire. This is the second death. And anyone not found written in the Book of Life was cast into the lake of fire.

-Revelation 20:10-15

"Anyone not found written in the Book of Life was cast into the lake of fire." Ladies and gentlemen, this is real, and it is serious. There is a beautiful reward for those who put their faith in Jesus to overcome the world by His Spirit. And there is an unthinkable punishment for those who do not.

19
THE ACTS OF THE APOSTLES

Well, as we've been examining what the New Testament has to say about the doctrine of holiness, we have now made it all the way to the end of the Bible, having just investigated the Revelation in the previous chapter. But since we began with Romans, it now remains to circle back to the beginning and see what the Gospels and Acts have to say on the matter. We'll tackle Acts first, and then close by exploring the Gospels.

Since Acts is a narrative, we should assume right off the bat that the kind of information we might be able to glean from the book about holiness will be quite different in its presentation, as compared with the epistles. In those letters, where Paul and the other apostles are giving direct teachings to the church, we find the most deliberate and intentional communication on this topic. By contrast, the narrative of Acts is given to us primarily to tell us a story about the events of the early church, not primarily to teach us how we as the later church should conduct ourselves.

Despite this, we can yet draw on Acts to support the doctrine of requisite holiness. In order to do just that, we will look at two features in the narrative: 1) the sermons of Acts and the appeals that conclude them, and 2) God's response to one unholy couple.

Repent

The book of Acts records several of the earliest Christian sermons ever delivered. Peter, Paul, and Stephen preached messages of personal testimony as well as Jewish history and the fulfillment of the promise of Abraham in the risen Christ. And at the end of these sermons, the preachers called on the hearers to do one thing: repent. The solution to their problems was not expressed primarily in terms of them changing their beliefs, but rather more commonly in terms of them changing their behavior.

First, Peter laid out the Gospel on the day of Pentecost. Those who heard his sermon were convicted and asked what they should do in response to the message. Peter said:

> Repent, and let every one of you be baptized in the name of Jesus Christ for the remission of sins; and you shall receive the gift of the Holy Spirit.
>
> -Acts 2:38

He didn't say "make sure you have a correct understanding of the Trinity and soteriology and Christology." He said *repent*, turn from evil and begin to do good by the power of the Spirit.

And he did not change the message in his next appearance, at Solomon's Porch. The people marveled that he and John were able to heal the lame man. This miracle afforded the apostles an opportunity to present the Gospel of Jesus as the impetus of that healing. It was by the power of the resurrected Christ that the man was healed, not by anything the men themselves had done. And Peter said in response:

> Repent therefore and be converted, that your sins may be blotted out, so that times of refreshing may come from the presence of the Lord.
>
> -Acts 3:19

Stephen comes next, boldly proclaiming the guilt of his audience for the murder of the "Righteous One." And he rebuked them, not so much for their thoughts and beliefs, as for their actions.

> You are always resisting the Holy Spirit. ... You received the law under the direction of angels and you have not kept it.
>
> -Acts 7:51b, 53 (CSB)

By contrast, Paul does close his sermon in Acts 13 by simply stating that "everyone who believes is justified" (13:39). His message to the Philippian jailer was similarly, "Believe on the Lord Jesus Christ, and you will be saved" (Acts 16:31). But his other sermons give more clarity to what is entailed by that *belief.* To the men of Athens he explained:

> God now commands all people everywhere to *repent*, because he has set a day when he is going to judge the world in righteousness by the man he has appointed.
>
> -Acts 17:30b-31a (CSB)

In Ephesus he recalled:

> I testified to both Jews and Greeks about *repentance* toward
> God and faith in our Lord Jesus.
>
> -Acts 20:21 (CSB)

And he claimed that the inheritance that God would one day
give to His people was reserved for:

> all those who are sanctified.
>
> -Acts 20:32

Thus, the consistent message of the apostles to those they were
evangelizing was that the way to get in right standing with God
was repentance, a turning away from their former ways, and a
turning toward God in all their acts.

Ananias and Sapphira

Perhaps no story in all of Scripture exemplifies God's
intolerance for sin any better than the story of Ananias and
Sapphira. Here in Acts 5, four chapters removed from the
ascension, three chapters removed from the outpouring of the
Holy Spirit at Pentecost, during the very dawn of the New
Covenant, we read about the judgment of the Lord upon a
couple who claim His name while yet operating outside His
standards.

> But a certain man named Ananias, with Sapphira his
> wife, sold a possession. And he kept back part of the
> proceeds, his wife also being aware of it, and brought a
> certain part and laid it at the apostles' feet. But Peter said,
> "Ananias, why has Satan filled your heart to lie to the Holy

Spirit and keep back part of the price of the land for yourself? While it remained, was it not your own? And after it was sold, was it not in your own control? Why have you conceived this thing in your heart? You have not lied to men but to God."

Then Ananias, hearing these words, fell down and breathed his last. So great fear came upon all those who heard these things. And the young men arose and wrapped him up, carried him out, and buried him.

Now it was about three hours later when his wife came in, not knowing what had happened. And Peter answered her, "Tell me whether you sold the land for so much?" She said, "Yes, for so much."

Then Peter said to her, "How is it that you have agreed together to test the Spirit of the Lord? Look, the feet of those who have buried your husband are at the door, and they will carry you out." Then immediately she fell down at his feet and breathed her last. And the young men came in and found her dead, and carrying her out, buried her by her husband. So great fear came upon all the church and upon all who heard these things.

-Acts 5:1-11

In the New Covenant. The covenant of grace. The covenant that we're still in today! God Himself slays these seemingly faithful churchgoers. And "great fear came upon all the church." What would it be like if our churches today were marked by such an appreciable fear of the Lord that we were loath to move one fraction beyond the boundary of righteous conduct? Is it possible that many of us in this "age of grace" are testing the Lord more often than we might think because we fail to recognize the severity of even our "negligible" transgressions? Thanks be to God that He has not chosen to make this kind of swift and immediate judgment normative for every sin. But this story should remind us that His posture toward all sin remains, and the judgment for unlamented, unpardoned sin remains to be meted out. Let us rededicate ourselves to walk circumspectly before Him from this day forward!

20
THE SYNOPTIC GOSPELS

Lately we've seen a trend among certain groups of nominal Christians, and that is the elevation of the Gospels above the Epistles, in terms of their authoritativeness. The apparent justification for this departure from orthodoxy can basically be summed up in the idea that the words of Jesus, as the Son of God, must certainly carry more weight than, say, the words of Paul, a mere man. I reject this premise, as well as the hermeneutical stance it leads to. Yes the words of Jesus are 100% inspired and true. But we believe that "All Scripture is given by inspiration of God" (2Ti 3:16), do we not? And so the words of Paul—those which are included in the Bible—are on par with the words of the Gospels.

Instead, those who would concentrate on the teachings of Jesus, almost to the exclusion of all other biblical texts, often begin to err in their doctrine-building by leaning heavily toward such characteristics of the Lord as His love, mercy, forgiveness, compassion, and grace. He certainly is the embodiment of all of these. But He exhibits some more dreadful characteristics as well. Without tempering the fake-Jesus of their imaginations with other balancing truths about God contained in Scripture, these folks blunder in a most disastrous way.

It is not my goal here to speak to these sects. But given this trend that certainly permeates Christendom in varying degrees across many traditions, I would like to turn now to the Gospels to see what they actually do say. *What if they were* our only authority? Could we prove the doctrine of requisite holiness based on the life and teachings of Jesus alone? Is Jesus only the Man of love and mercy? And did He teach belief-alone as the way to salvation? Or did He teach belief-in-action as the way? What does Jesus have to say about holiness? We'll find out right now, beginning in this chapter with the so-called synoptic Gospels of Matthew Mark, and Luke; and ending with the Gospel of John in the next.

Repent and Follow

There's no doubt that Jesus tells us that we are saved by "believing in Him." It's foundational to Christianity, and the core of our most beloved verse, John 3:16. But what does it mean to believe in Him? And is that the only word that Jesus used to describe the process of conversion? Well, no it isn't. In fact, more often than not Jesus used words like *repent* and *follow* to describe our pathway out of sin and condemnation.

Before Jesus' ministry began, his predecessor, John the Baptist, preached a message of repentance. His first words recorded in Scripture were, "Repent, for the kingdom of heaven is at hand" (Mat 3:2). Now note the first words recorded of Jesus' ministry. He came out from the wilderness of trials, and

> From that time Jesus began to preach and to say, "Repent,
> for the kingdom of heaven is at hand."
>
> -Matthew 4:17

Identical! He did not say *believe*; he said *repent*. "From that time,"
in other words it was not just a one-time message, but rather it
was His consistent message throughout His ministry. We have
confirmation of this from the book of the Revelation, for we
saw there that Jesus was still speaking to the churches the
message of repentance, even after His ascension.

Not only was this His message, but it became the message of
His own disciples. When He sent them out in pairs to spread the
news about Him,

> ...they went out and preached that people should repent.
>
> -Mark 6:12

The other word Jesus frequently used to teach us how to be
saved was *follow*. When He called His disciples, He did not say
"believe in Me," He said, "follow me." He instructed the rich
young ruler in the same way.

> "You still lack one thing. Sell all that you have and
> distribute to the poor, and you will have treasure in heaven;
> and come, follow Me."
>
> -Luke 18:22b

And in both cases—the disciples and the rich young ruler—we
learn that implicit in the phrase "follow me" is the forsaking of
all worldly possessions and relationships. The disciples were
willing to do that; the rich young ruler was not. Now we should
not interpret that, in today's world, to mean that we should close

our bank accounts and forsake our families. Rather, it simply means that no earthly relationship and no earthly possession has priority in our lives over Him. Our money belongs to Him, and we must be willing to part with as much of it as He asks us for. And our relationships do not stand in the way of His plans and desires; we have to be willing to discard any relationship that adversely affects our Christian walk.

The Fruit of Repentance

Not only did Jesus teach that repentance is the way to salvation, but He also taught that those who walk in repentance will show evidence of a life well lived, bearing fruit consistent with their testimony.

> "For a good tree does not bear bad fruit, nor does a bad tree bear good fruit. For every tree is known by its own fruit."
>
> -Luke 6:43-44a

You cannot claim to be a good tree (a.k.a. Christian) if you're producing bad fruit (a.k.a. sin). It just doesn't work that way. Right after that, Jesus goes on to say:

> "But why do you call Me 'Lord, Lord,' and do not do the things which I say?"
>
> -Luke 6:46

It doesn't make any sense that you would claim Jesus as *Lord* (that is to say, *slave master*), and yet not do what He says. By definition, if He is your Lord, you must do what He says. Your fruit is simply not consistent with your testimony if you don't. Here is what the difference amounts to:

> "Whoever comes to Me, and hears My sayings and does them, I will show you whom he is like: He is like a man building a house, who dug deep and laid the foundation on the rock. And when the flood arose, the stream beat vehemently against that house, and could not shake it, for it was founded on the rock. But he who heard and did nothing is like a man who built a house on the earth without a foundation, against which the stream beat vehemently; and immediately it fell. And the ruin of that house was great."
>
> -Luke 6:47-49

You are ruined if you do not actually do what He says, if you do not actually live a life that is empowered by His Spirit to be pleasing to Him.

In a similar passage Jesus very clearly states that those who do not have the fruit to back up the claim of salvation will not see Him.

> "Not everyone who says to Me, 'Lord, Lord,' shall enter the kingdom of heaven, but he who does the will of My Father in heaven. "Many will say to Me in that day, 'Lord, Lord, have we not prophesied in your name, cast out demons in Your name, and done many wonders in Your name?' And then I will declare to them, 'I never knew you; depart from Me, you who practice lawlessness!'"
>
> -Matthew 7:21-23

When it comes to salvation, it's not the gifts of the Spirit but the fruit of the Spirit that counts. He can give you a gift to use for the benefit of others, and still not be Lord of your life. But when you surrender yourself to His will so that fruit is produced within you, then your "Lord, Lord" will be validated.

The Crucified Life

Jesus takes us one step further by suggesting that following Him as Lord actually means our own crucifixion, that is the death of our flesh. And not just any death. It is a torturous and exacting process to submit to the subjugation of the flesh. It demands that a man "deny himself, and take up his cross daily, and follow" the Lord (Luke 9:23).

A Higher Standard

The proponents of "sloppy grace" basically hold that the standard of conduct is lower in the New Covenant than in the Old. God was harsh and judgmental in the old system, but He is loving and merciful in the new. So whereas sin in the Old Testament required animal sacrifice, or in some cases was even met with the death penalty, sins (of the past, present, and future) in the New Testament are covered by the blood of Jesus, and require nothing more than a half-hearted "I'm sorry" directed toward the Lord.

Well, once again, this view is not faithful to Scripture as a whole. We certainly don't go around chopping off hands and stoning people nowadays. But those serious sins, if they're never repented of, will be judged one day. And according to Jesus' teaching, the standard of conduct in the New Covenant is not lower than the Old, but in fact, higher!

Speaking in His sermon on the mount, He says, "Do not think that I came to destroy the Law or the Prophets. I did not come to destroy but to fulfill" (Matt 5:17). Then he presents a series of teachings marked by the phrase, "You have heard that it was said … but I say to you." In other words, the old system teaches one thing, but My new system teaches another. And we find in every case that the standard is higher in the new system.

"You have heard that it was said to those of old, 'You shall not murder, and whoever murders will be in danger of the judgment.' But I say to you that whoever is angry with his brother without a cause shall be in danger of the judgment."

-Matthew 5:21-22a

"You have heard that it was said to those of old, 'You shall not commit adultery.' But I say to you that whoever looks at a woman to lust for her has already committed adultery with her in his heart."

-Matthew 5:27-28

"Furthermore it has been said, 'Whoever divorces his wife, let him give her a certificate of divorce.' But I say to you that whoever divorces his wife for any reason except sexual immorality causes her to commit adultery; and whoever marries a woman who is divorced commits adultery."

-Matthew 5:31-32

"You have heard that it was said, 'An eye for an eye and a tooth for a tooth.' But I tell you not to resist an evil person. But whoever slaps you on your right cheek, turn the other also."

-Matthew 5:38-39

"You have heard that it was said, 'You shall love your neighbor and hate your enemy.' But I say to you, love your enemies, bless those who curse you, do good to those who hate you, and pray for those who spitefully use you and persecute you, that you may be sons of your Father in heaven"

-Matthew 5:43-45a

New Covenant living is about being upstanding and above reproach and holy, not about being excited that we can get away with as much as possible.

The Severity of Sin

Not only is the standard of conduct higher in the New Covenant, the level of diligence and consecration we are to maintain in our fight against sin is higher! So calamitous are the consequences of sin that Jesus teaches:

> "If your hand or foot causes you to sin, cut it off and cast it from you. It is better for you to enter into life lame or maimed, rather than having two hands or two feet, to be cast into the everlasting fire. And if your eye causes you to sin, pluck it out and cast it from you. It is better for you to enter into life with one eye, rather than having two eyes, to be cast into hell fire."
>
> -Matthew 18:8-9

Now, is Jesus actually suggesting that we dismember ourselves? No, He would rather us simply repent and cry out for mercy, and turn from sin and begin to live a life that pleases Him. So, plucking out your eye is not your first tactic. God has provided a better way. Still the fact remains, if the only choice were between sinning and losing some body parts, losing the body parts is the preferred option.

21
THE GOSPEL OF JOHN

Our final study will focus on John's gospel. John, as compared with the other gospel writers, is more concerned with helping us to understand who Jesus is than he is with helping us to understand what He did. Much of our Christology is taken from John for this reason. John also maintains an emphasis on *believing* as the means of salvation, throughout His writing. For this reason it would be particularly important if we were able to pick up from John some additional teaching on the necessity of holiness. When John tells us—and when Jesus tells us, in John's writings—that *believing* is all that is needed to be saved, do they mean belief without action? Or do they mean the kind of belief that is evidenced by a life change?

Believe, to Practice

To answer that question, let's turn first to John 3. This chapter, of course, records Jesus' famous conversation with Nicodemus, in which He famously states that eternal life is granted to those who *believe* (John 3:16). But it's the portion after this verse that interests us here because it adds depth to our understanding of what exactly Jesus meant when he said *believe*.

> "Anyone who believes in him is not condemned, but anyone who does not believe is already condemned, because he has not believed in the name of the one and only Son of God. This is the judgment: The light has come into the world, and people loved darkness rather than the light because their deeds were evil. For everyone who does evil hates the light and avoids it, so that his deeds may not be exposed. But anyone who lives by the truth comes to the light, so that his works may be shown to be accomplished by God."
>
> -John 3:18-21 (CSB)

Jesus clearly states that *believing* is the key to receiving *no condemnation*. But then He states, "this is the judgment," in other words, this is the nature of that condemnation: people choose darkness over light. And their deeds are evil. Notice, it's not evil beliefs that He's drawing attention to, it's evil deeds. The reason evildoers hate the light is because, deep down in their hearts, they simply don't want to be exposed. They don't want to change, they don't want to repent. If they allow the light to bring up before their eyes the areas where they're wrong, they'll have to deal with those areas. And they don't want to. But those with a pure heart, those who truly seek truth and love God, they embrace the light because they want their impurities to be discovered and eradicated so they can be holy and without blemish. And their "works" are shown to be accomplished by God. In the end, these believers, these who are not condemned, still do works.

Condemnation or life. Those are the only two options. And Jesus is actually the One who is given authority to judge who is given life and who earns condemnation.

> "For as the Father has life in Himself, so He has granted the Son to have life in Himself, and has given Him authority to execute judgment also, because He is the Son of Man. Do not marvel at this; for the hour is coming in which all who are in the graves will hear His voice and come forth—those who have done good, to the resurrection of life, and those who have done evil, to the resurrection of condemnation."
>
> -John 5:26-29

This passage begins with a reiteration of the principle of believing in order to have everlasting life (5:24), but it ends by drawing a corollary between our deeds and our rewards. "Those who have *done* good" and "those who have *done* evil." You cannot simply *believe*, without going on to *do good!*

Jesus states this plainly later on in the gospel. Speaking to those who "believed in Him," He says:

> "If you continue in my word, you really are my disciples."
>
> -John 8:31b (CSB)

If you *continue*. A true saving faith in Christ will show evidence of continuation in a life of dedication to Him.

Sin is Not Tolerated by Jesus

The Pharisees chided Jesus for His association with sinners. If we're not careful we can get the idea that because Jesus associated with sinners, He condoned sinful behavior. Or more likely we might think that He's there to "take care of their problem," so therefore He's not bothered by their sin, and it's not a big deal. Nothing could be further from the truth. Jesus explained his tactics by noting that it's sick people who need a doctor (Mark 2:17). Jesus thought of sinners as sick people. It was not ok with Him that they were sinning. And it's actually all the more stunning that He would associate with them, considering their condition, and considering that it was their sin that would eventually drive Him to His death.

In the story of the man healed at the pool of Bethesda, we learn that sin is not acceptable to Jesus, and it comes at a price. After Jesus healed the man, He later found him in the temple and said to him:

> "See, you have been made well. Sin no more, lest a worse thing come upon you."
>
> -John 5:14b

The man is told in no uncertain terms to stop sinning, because sinning is contrary to what pleases God. And he is told that if he does not stop sinning, something will happen to him that is worse than physical paralysis. From our knowledge of Scripture as a whole, we know that that worse thing is no less than eternal damnation. Yes, Jesus associated with sinners, but it was for the purpose of loving them out of sin and into repentance.

A Final Word on Fruit

We saw that the concept of *fruit* became fairly significant in Paul's explanations of what the Christian life should look like. He laid out for us the dimensions of spiritual fruit—love, joy, peace, and so on—in Galatians 5; and he said in Romans 6 that our fruit *is holiness.*

In John 15, Jesus also addresses the concept of *fruit.* He explains that *we should* bear fruit. He tells us *the way* to bear fruit, which is abiding in Him. And He informs us of the sobering *consequence for failure* to bear fruit.

> "I am the true vine, and My Father is the vinedresser. Every branch in Me that does not bear fruit He takes away; and every branch that bears fruit He prunes, that it may bear more fruit. You are already clean because of the word which I have spoken to you. Abide in Me, and I in you. As the branch cannot bear fruit of itself, unless it abides in the vine, neither can you, unless you abide in Me.
>
> I am the vine, you are the branches. He who abides in Me, and I in him, bears much fruit; for without Me you can do nothing. If anyone does not abide in Me, he is cast out as a branch and is withered; and they gather them and throw them into the fire, and they are burned."
>
> -John 15:1-6

Once again, we know from Paul's writings that our fruit is holiness. So let's recap this passage with that in mind. Everyone who does not walk in holiness (does not bear fruit), He "takes away." But those who are holy He prunes, so that they will be even more holy. We cannot achieve holiness in and of ourselves, but only by abiding in the Holy One. To *abide in* is to live continually in. In other words to abide is to be *engrossed in God.* We've captured this thought several times now, but it's worth going over one more time. What are our minds set on? Are we engrossed in ourselves? Are we engrossed in the world? Are you abiding in Him? Are you engrossed in Him? Or are you abiding in something else? The way to holiness, the way to bearing fruit, is abiding in Him.

Finally, we get this warning. Those branches that do not abide in Him are cast out and withered, gathered together, thrown into the fire, and burned. Friend, don't let it be you. Continue on in Him, walk in holiness, avoid this dreadful fate and persevere to claim your imperishable crown!

Responding to the Adultress: A Final Parable

As we come to a close, I would like to examine one final statement of Jesus. It's not exactly a teaching, and yet it offers us perhaps the most concise and complete encapsulation of our thesis in all of Scripture. It is His response to the woman caught in adultery.

The Scribes and Pharisees had brought this woman to Jesus to test Him so that they might find some reason to bring accusation against Him. Of course, He responded, in His most masterful way, by turning the subject of sin back on to the accusers. "For all have sinned and fall short of the glory of God"—so to speak. The leaders reluctantly turn and walk away, leaving only Jesus and the woman to arrive at a verdict. Jesus asks rhetorically whether anyone remains to condemn her, to which she replies that there is no one. Now notice Jesus' tripartite reply:

"Neither do I condemn you;
go
and sin no more."

-John 8:11b

We began this book by looking carefully at Romans 8:1. We end it by looking at how Jesus articulates the same truth. Let's note together the correlation:

Paul writes: "There is therefore now no condemnation to those who are in Christ Jesus"
Jesus expresses the same thought: "Neither do I condemn you"

Paul writes: "walk"
Jesus expresses the same thought: "go"

Paul writes: "not according to the flesh, but according to the Spirit"
Jesus expresses the same thought: "and sin no more"

There is no condemnation for those who walk not according to the flesh but according to the Spirit. There is no condemnation for those who go and sin no more. *In exchange for repentance, total submission and obedience, believing in Him to empower you by His Spirit to live a life that is free from sin and pleasing to Him; Jesus Christ offers you no condemnation.* That is the message of Jesus. That is the message of Paul. That is the message of John the Baptist. That is the message of the Apostles. That is the message of the entire New Testament. That is the message of salvation. That is the message. Holiness is Not Optional.

EPILOGUE:
IF ANYONE DOES SIN

I realize this book is heavy. It has to be heavy to counter-balance the preponderance of featherweight preaching in the American Church today. It is only because I have aimed to strangle the "sloppy grace" doctrine that I have leaned so strongly to the judgment side of God here. The fact is, even though holiness is not optional, it is not the first thing or even the most important thing that God requires. First He wants your love. He wants you to seek Him and know Him and rest and be comforted, as a son in a Father's care. He doesn't just want you to obey the rules, He wants you to *want* to obey the rules because you have a heart that desires to please Him.

If you truly want to be right and do right, if you truly desire for Him to burn out the impurities of your life, if you continually submit and repent when you know you've done wrong, He *will* do the work of sanctification in your life. And if you do sin, your repentant heart will be met with compassion and forgiveness. Because the fact is, *grace is not sloppy, but mercy is.*

When I say *grace is not sloppy*, what I mean is—and what I've spent an entire book explaining is—you can't just go through life with a flippant attitude toward God and His ways, and then appeal to His grace to "cover" your shortcomings. But when I say *mercy is sloppy*, what I mean is, if you humble yourself and truly recognize your low and pitiable state, repenting and crying out to Him for mercy, *it will always be there!*

The apostle John wrote of this endless supply of mercy in his first epistle:

> ...if anyone does sin, we have an advocate with the Father—Jesus Christ the righteous one.
> -1 John 2:1b (CSB)

> If we confess our sins, He is faithful and just to forgive us our sins and to cleanse us from all unrighteousness.
> -1 John 1:9

God is good. God is merciful. He desires for every sinner to repent and be revealed as His adopted son, newly entitled to an inheritance of eternal life and infinite joy in Him. He desires for every believer to turn fully to Him, to be born again and walk in repentance, persevering to the end. If you belong to Him, He is for you. And if you don't belong to Him, He wants to be for you. Either way, He's not out to get you. Not yet anyway. There is a judgment day, and on that day it will be too late; if you're not His on that day, He will most certainly be against you. But that day is not today. That day hasn't come yet. Today, He is waiting, full of mercy, ready to welcome you to His family and to begin to empower you to live a victorious life.

NOTES

[1] Edwin A. Blum, "Study Notes on Romans," in *HCSB Study Bible* (Nashville: Holman Bible Publishers, 2010), 1938.

[2] John Wesley, "On Sin in Believers," in *The Sermons of John Wesley: A Collection for the Christian Journey*, ed. Kenneth K. Collins and Jason E. Vickers (Nashville: Abingdon Press, 2013), 565.

[3] All definitions of biblical terms given in this book are adaptations of the *Brown-Driver-Briggs* and *Gesenius* lexicons, both of which are available for free from various online sources. Francis Brown 1894-1916, *The Brown, Driver, Briggs Hebrew and English Lexicon: with an Appendix Containing the Biblical Aramaic: Coded with the Numbering System from Strong's Exhaustive Concordance of the Bible* (Peabody, MA: Hendrickson Publishers, 1996); Wilhelm Gesenius and Samuel Prideaux Tregelles, *Gesenius' Hebrew and Chaldee Lexicon to the Old Testament Scriptures* (Grand Rapids, MI: Eerdmans, 1957).

Made in the USA
Las Vegas, NV
05 April 2023

70223046R00095